Kornfeld

George 323   938-7023

THE *GREATEST* BOOK OF POKER FOR WINNERS!

The Four Basic Rules and Strategies for Winning at Poker

Written for the beginning poker player
as well as seasoned players
who want to increase their winnings
and enjoyment of seven-card stud and Texas hold'em. . .

by George Epstein

with special chapters on
The Psychology of Poker
and
Rules and Strategies for Texas Hold'em
by Dr. Daniel E. Abrams

Third Printing; Upgraded; October 2003

Published by T/C PRESS
Los Angeles, California

First Edition; Third Printing/Upgraded October 2003

Library of Congress Cataloging-in-Publication Data:
TX 5-495-727; April 6, 2001
George Epstein
The Greatest Book of Poker for Winners!

ISBN 0-938-64843-8

Artwork by Anita Klebanoff

Printed in the United States of America
10 9 8 7 6 5 4 3 2 1

This book is dedicated to the most
important people in my life:
My mother and father,
Esther and Eli Epstein (deceased);
My wife, Irene (deceased);
My son, David (deceased);
My wonderful daughter, Sue;
My beautiful granddaughters,
Dani and Esther Epstein;
My talented and loving ladyfriend,
Anita Klebanoff;
My maternal grandparents, Sarah and
Julius Hecht (deceased);
and also to the man who taught me the
difference between playing poker and
playing WINNING poker, my very
good friend Phil Treiger (deceased).

So you want to be a millionaire!

Why not?   That's an understandable goal. . .
Yes, you can achieve that goal playing poker
by using the Basic Poker Rules and Strategies
described in this book.

But. . . *read on and you will find out how.*

* * *

Thou Shall. . .

Just as some of thy neighbors may at
times violate the Ten Commandments,
so too thou may be prone, on occasion,
to deviate from the Basic Poker Rules.
Fear not. Thou will neither suffer the
wrath of the Lord nor that of any group
in our land. Thou hast violated no
punishable law of man or of nature --
only thine own opportunity to
WIN MORE OFTEN & WIN MORE $.

-- George Epstein

It's great fun to be a winner!

GREATEST
THE ∧ BOOK OF POKER FOR WINNERS!

CONTENTS

Chapter 1 -- Introduction 1
- Essential Characteristics of a Winner 4
- What are the Special Characteristics of
  a Winning Poker Player? 10
    PokerSharks Versus PokerPigeons;
    and Tortoises Versus. Hares
- Why Do We Want to be Winning
  Poker Players? 13
- Playing Seven-Card Stud 14
    The Stakes.
    Five Cards Determine the Winning Hand
    Antes
    The Poker Table
    The Deal
    Cautions
    Betting and Raising
    Going All In
    Variations Among Poker Casinos
    The House's Rake
    Why I Prefer No-Ante Games
- Why Play Poker 30
- Yes, You Can Become a Millionaire! 32
- What Beats? 36
- Poker Room Regulations 43
- A Little on Statistics 50

Life is NOT a bowl of cherries. Life IS really like a poker game!

Chapter 2 -- The Four Basic Poker Rules for Winning   52

- <u>Rule #1</u>: Set Your Goal and Limits;
  Use Money Management
- <u>Rule #2</u>: Carefully Select Both the Game and
  Table at Which You Play
    - Selecting the Game of Poker to Play
    - Selecting the Table
    - *-- Are There Enough PokerPigeons?*
    - What About a "Home" Game?
    - What About Table Position?
- <u>Rule #3</u>: Don't Lose! — Play Only Those Hands
  You Have a Good Chance of Winning
- <u>Rule #4</u>: Be Alert
- Comments

It takes PERSONAL DISCIPLINE to be a winner!

Chapter 3 -- Poker Strategies for Winners:
How to Win More Often and Win More $ 121

- What Do We Mean When We Speak of
  a Strategy for Winning at Poker?
- Developing the Poker Strategies for Winning
- The Nine Key Poker Strategies   125
    - Strategy #1: Raising on an Opening Pair
      -- An Important Exception to Poker Strategy #1
    - Strategy #2: Playing With
      a Marginal Opening Hand
    - Strategy #3: Starting With Three-of-a-Kind
    - Strategy #4: Betting After the Fourth Card
    - Strategy #5: Playing Two-Pair Hands
      -- The Conservative Strategy
      -- Epstein's More Aggressive Strategy
    - Strategy #6: Raising With Two Pair
    - Strategy #7: Playing Aggressively
      the Right Way
    - Strategy #8: Playing Against Aggressive Opponents
    - Strategy #9: Bluffing Strategy

It "pays" to be prepared. . .

Chapter 4 -- Poker Strategies for Special Situations   189
- Observing Your Neighbor's Hole Cards
- Using "Tells"   (The Science of Kinesics)
  -- *Watch What He is "Telling" You Without
  Using Words*
- Strategy on Card-Tracking
- Strategy for Betting on the River
- Raising with the Best Hand on the River
- Drinking While Playing Poker;
  Your Mental and Physical State

You can make your life a Royal Flush!

Chapter 5 -- Rules and Strategies for Texas Hold'em   219
- Structure of the Game
- Special House Regulations for Texas Hold'em
- The Basic Poker Rules Applied to Texas Hold'em
  -- Starting Hand Values
- Strategies for Texas Hold'em
  -- Strategies for Pre-Flop Betting
  -- Post-Flop Strategy
  -- Bluffing
  -- Advanced Strategies for Texas Hold'em

Winning isn't everything, but losing isn't anything. -- Jesse Unruh

Chapter 6 -- The Psychology of Poker   241
- Five Key Factors
- Important Personality Characteristics
- How to Assess Your Opponents
- Moving Up
- Don't Blame the Dealer
- A Mistake in Poker is Not Always a Mistake
- Compulsive Gambling

Laugh a lot. A good sense of humor cures almost all life's ills.
-- H. Jackson Brown, Jr..

Chapter 7 -- Making An Allowance for Antes; Recommendations for Tipping/Showing Your Appreciation   281

- How Should Antes Affect Your Playing?
- Recommendations for Tipping

Luck comes and goes; but knowledge stays forever.
      -- Bill Burton; About.com Casino Gambling Guide

Chapter 8 -- For Senior Citizens: Playing Poker for Fun, $, and Good Health   288

- How to Live Longer and Healthier by Participating in Mentally and Physically Challenging Activities
- And What About Physical Health
- And It's Fun Too!

We don't stop playing because we grow old;
we grow old because we stop playing.
      -- George Bernard Shaw

APPENDIX -- Folding Hands for Texas Hold'em   298

➤ _____ ➤

It's about LUCK. Who said it first?

The harder we work, the luckier we get.
      -- Vince Lombardi

I'm a great believer in luck,
and I find the harder I work the more I have of it.
      -- Thomas Jefferson

It's always fun to win!

FOREWORD

Poker is more than a game of chance. It is more than a game to match your skills against those of others. It is more than an opportunity to win some money -- or whatever the rewards may be. In fact, the game of poker is really a microcosm of life. Learning to play <u>winning</u> poker can help you to become success-ful in your life. . .

Succeeding in the game of poker -- winning -- requires one to abide by a set of basic rules and apply key strategies. The same is true in life. Certainly there is an element of luck; but, in the final analysis, winning -- or succeeding -- is based on how well one learns and applies the basic rules and strategies.

What is success? Why do we all strive for success? There is more to life than "earning a living." The enjoyment of one's life and achieving success are closely intertwined. What does winning at the game of poker have to do with succeeding in life?

This book explains how to become a winner at the game of poker based on my poker "education" and engineering experi-ence, extending over many years. I leave it to you, the reader, to apply this to playing poker and to your own life.

The greatest contribution to my poker education was the teachings of a dear, now-deceased friend, Phil Treiger, a man who had many remarkable abilities -- not the least of which was how to win at poker. He was also extremely successful as an out-standing surgeon, businessman and philanthropist.

My poker "education" goes back to my childhood days, watching my parents play penny-ante poker around the kitchen table; and I participated in many a game while attending college and in the service during World War II -- even on the high seas in the "comfort" of the ship's cramped radio shack.

In my teen-age years, I played poker to win picture cards of the major league baseball players. Oh, how I treasured these.

After having been re-introduced to the game by the late Phil Treiger, I studied numerous books written by experts to get further pointers and ideas. And I played frequently -- actually "studied" to gain on-the-job experience -- at various poker rooms in Las Vegas, Lake Tahoe, and in card clubs in the Los Angeles area. There I honed my skills and developed the four Basic Poker Rules and the series of Poker Strategies presented in this book.

Key to developing these rules and strategies was my many years of experience as an engineer in the aerospace industry. Engineers like to reduce problems to their simplest elements. They try to create order out of chaos -- most of the time. Engineers try to create simple, orderly systems out of chaotic situations. During my introduction to "winning poker," I had learned many "do's and don'ts" about playing the game of poker -- a literal plethora of things to remember! In fact, it was practically mind-boggling: *Do this; don't do that...* How could anyone, other than perhaps a "professional" poker player, keep track of all these "do's and don'ts" -- especially while immersed in and playing under the pressure of a real game of poker? It was difficult, to say the least...

Then I realized that I could make good use of my training as an engineer. I transformed this vast sea -- more like a tidal wave -- of "do's and don'ts" into two parts: (1) a simple set of four Basic Poker Rules -- what you must do if you want to win most of the time, and (2) a series of Poker Strategies that will help you to win more often and more money ($) when you do win.

To prove the effectiveness of these Basic Poker Rules, almost as an experiment, my wife and I introduced our daughter, Sue, to the game. She had never before played poker. She now wins most of the time! One dealer at a Las Vegas poker room told me that Sue is an excellent player -- "better than you are!" he said. The reason: She follows the rules religiously, whereas I too often will deviate for one reason or another.

As I became more adept at playing poker, simultaneously pursuing my career in engineering -- quite successfully, I would add -- I realized that there is a strong correlation between winning at poker and achieving success during one's life. Of course! And the more I thought about it, the more I realized that one could apply the Basic Poker Rules and the concept of strategies for winning at poker to achieve success during one's life.

Lee Iacocca's autobiography suggests that he had discovered the connection between winning at poker and succeeding in life:

"I gave up sports and started playing chess, bridge, and especially poker. I still love poker, and I usually win. It's a great game for learning when to exploit an advantage, when to back off, and when to bluff. (It sure came in handy years later during tough union negotiations!)"
-- Quoting Lee Iacocca from his autobiography, in describing his school days; published by Bantam Books; 1984.

In the final analysis, it is winning -- in both the games of poker and life -- that is exciting and self-satisfying. My dear, now-deceased wife's reaction while I was first writing this book, was: *"Winning is exhilarating!"*

This book has been written (1) to aid the beginning poker player -- as my daughter was -- to become a winner; and (2) to be of value to experienced poker players who want to improve their playing and enjoyment of the game. In addition to explaining the Basic Poker Rules and Poker Strategies, many terms that are familiar to most poker players are defined, and examples are presented to help the reader understand the various concepts described. Equally important, being an engineer, I realize that you can best learn and apply the Basic Poker Rules and Poker Strategies if these are clearly explained, including the rationale for each. The better you understand these, the easier it will be to apply them during the "heat of battle." Yes, the poker table is very much like a battlefield; and you are out there to best your opponents -- "the enemy" (friendly ones, I hope) in a figurative, not literal, sense.

To further attest to the value of these four relatively simple Basic Poker Rules for winning at poker, there is the story of the young woman who attended a professional society meeting at which I gave a talk on "Poker -- Success -- Life!" At the end of my talk, she asked me for a copy of the vugraph charts with my four Basic Poker Rules. A few months later I happened to see her; she came over to me and thanked me for my help. She had twice visited Las Vegas since my talk; and, using the Basic Poker Rules, she had come away a winner both times! She was delighted.

And finally, I want to say that it is important in playing poker -- as in the game of life -- to have a sense of humor. Don't take yourself or your opponents, or the game of poker, too seriously. After all, in the final analysis, life is so short. Enjoy it to the fullest while you are able; but plan and be prepared for the future too. Toward this end, along the way as you read this book, you will find some humorous comments and sayings. Enjoy them. You may want to use some of them. Be my guest.

-- George Epstein

To acquire knowledge, one must study;
but to acquire wisdom, one must observe.
-- Anonymous

ACKNOWLEDGMENTS

A special "Thank You" to June Field, publisher of *Poker Digest* magazine, for her "well-beyond-the-call-of-duty" efforts in helping me in writing this book.

So many people have contributed to this book in so many ways that it may not be possible for me to acknowledge all of them; surely, I am bound to forget some. *One of the advantages for me of being a senior citizen is that I can blame my age for any memory lapse.*

There were many who contributed without realizing it -- perhaps by setting an example for me, or making a significant point during a conversation, or during a poker game, or even during a business meeting. Certainly my parents and many teachers fit into this category. We are all the products of our upbringing, education and training, the environment in which we live, our inherited characteristics, and our culture. All of these and, concomitantly, the people associated with these have contributed in some way to this book. In addition to those to whom this book is dedicated, there are a number of people whose names come to mind:

Heidi and Dan Abrams; Ed Ames; Bill Bandaruk; Jerry Bauer; Bob Bendarzewski;* Richard Blyth; Ed Bobak; Sam Brelant;* Milt Buck;* Miss Burke (my fourth-grade teacher);* Ed Bushman; Mrs. Buxbaum;* Mr. "Bunky" Cannell (high-school teacher)* Rose and Ted Cardonsky;* Phyllis and Mike Caro; Mike Clark; Leslie Cohen; Mort Cole;* Saul Cooper; Norm Crosby; Dan Daniels;* John Delmonte;* Bill Dewar;* Prof. A. G. H. Dietz;* Dolores Donovan; Ken Drake; Miss Driscoll (my seventh grade teacher);* Barry Evans; Ginny Fahey; Prof. R. J. Fessenden;* Mike Feuer; Seymour Feuerstein; Mel Foster; Jerry Friden; Ruthanne and George Friedman; Janice Gershlak; Vivian and Max Gold;* Jack Goldberg; Stan Goldin; Audrey and Harvey* Goldstein; Bernie Goldware; Charlie Hamermesh;* Gary Hawkins; Gene Hertler; Carrie Hodes;* Jack Jones; Bob Josephson; Arthur Karas;* Irv Katz;* Ron Keyson; Sheri and Hamid Khatami; Lenny Knazik;* Christine Konecny;* Joanne and Jeff* Kravitz; Ursula Kronheim;* Ed Laird; Frances and Harry Lavidor;* Paula and Steve Lavidor; Henry Lee; Stu Lee; Lorraine and Sam Lefkowitz; Betty and Ed* Levenstein; Walt Leverton; Kitty and Luckie Levine;* Herbert Levine; Sid Litvack; Joe MacLean; Robert Mann; Prof. Herman Mark;* Jewel and Paul Markell; Andy Marshall; Eric Marx;* Irene Master; Jim McClelland;*

Marty Milden; "Rusty" Miller; John Moricoli;* Ed Morris; Joan and Don Nadler; Max Nadler;* Kris Neville;* Eric Niven; Mr. O'Donnell (high-school teacher);* Ida and Mac Okstein;* Dr. Gene Oppenheim; Leah Pasman;* Sonya and Eddie* Passy; Eunice and Harry Patick;* Arnold Paddock; Enold Pierre-Louis; Allen Prince; Larry Rachal; Jan and Bill Riley; Prof. Walter S. Ritchie;* Bill Rozance;* Flo and Marv Rosenfeld;* Joel Rothberg; Lou Rubin;* Ed Rucks;* Susan Ruth; Mr. and Mrs. Rutskin;* Ray Saldonis; Linda Sauter; Seymour Schwartz;* Howard Schwartz; Dom Scrooc; Esther Seifer;* Harold Seifer; Helen Sherman; Susan Shlanger; Al Siegel;* Bob Silberberg;* Sam Silberkraus;* Stuart Simon; Bernice and Hal Smallen;* Prof. J. Harold Smith;* Fred Spiegl; Jack Springer;* Wilma and Vic Stern; Norman Stone;* Frances and Morris Tabrisky;* Ruby Tabrisky;* Lou Tallman;* Bill Tobin; Jim Toner; Honey Treiger;* Arnold Tuckerman;* Lee and Jack Weissman; Leona White; Toby Willner; Lois Wolff;* Marge and Ted Wolff; Dr. Stanley Zemer; Frieda and Charlie Zimmerman;* Sally and Harry Zimon;* my very special uncles, Harold, Benny, Irving, and Arthur Hecht;* my sister, Phyllis, and her husband, Al Rotman; and my nephews, Michael and Steve Rotman

--George Epstein

---

* Deceased

⮞ _____ ⮞

Great advice for everyone:

Smiles are nice.
They make you so gay.
They make you smile too.
And they make everyone smile
in the whole world.

-- Dani Epstein, aged 5 yr. and 11 mos. (January 18, 1997)

THE **GREATEST** BOOK OF POKER FOR WINNERS!

CHAPTER ONE -- INTRODUCTION

> *The clock of life is wound but once*
> *And no man has the power*
> *To tell just when the hands will stop*
> *On what day -- or what hour*
> *Now is the only time you have*
> *So live it with a will*
> *Don't wait until tomorrow*
> *The hands may then be still.*
> --Author unknown

The game of poker has been played around the world for many centuries. It is presumed to have been introduced about 1000 years ago by the ancient Persians under the name *"nas."* The present technique of betting was introduced in France during the 16th century; and, shortly after, the concept of bluffing is believed to have been introduced in England.

1

Fortunes have been won and lost in a poker game. And people have been killed over a game of poker -- especially if caught cheating. Poker played a significant role in the settling of the West in the U.S. Today, the game is played for fun, profit, and challenge by more and more people all over the world. It even has been rumored that the game of poker has been used by politicians and businessmen as a means to "purchase" influence.

Philosophically, winning at the game of poker is a form of success. When you come away from the table as a winner, you have achieved a goal of sorts and thereby attained success. Certainly, winning at a game of poker ought not be likened to succeeding in one's life in terms of the magnitude of its importance. On the other hand, learning to win at the game of poker can be applied to succeeding in life.

There are four -- just four -- fundamental and essential "poker laws" that I prescribe which are absolutely necessary for winning at poker. These apply wherever you engage in the game of poker. We will refer to these as the Basic Poker Rules. I call these RULES, because they are guides or principles for governing action. Akin to laws, you <u>must</u> obey these rules if you want to be a winner. If you understand and follow these rules, you are bound to win in the long run. You will not win every time you sit down at the poker table. No one can. But, if you properly use the Basic Poker Rules, you are assured of winning most of the time -- in the long run. There is an element of luck. Indeed, in the short run, luck is a significant part of any gambling game. Over a long period of time, the occurrences of good and bad luck should tend to even out -- more or less like a ragged sine wave. But, by following our Basic Poker Rules, you can be certain that you will win more often than not -- perhaps two-thirds of the time; more often if you are "running" in good luck. But bear in mind that there will be occasions when, even while you play properly by the rules, luck will run against you -- and you will lose. Hopefully, those occasions will be relatively rare. But "Lady Luck" can be fickle. Your objective should be to optimize your winnings when enjoying "good luck," and minimize your losses when suffering a period of "bad luck."

An example of the element of luck: Playing seven-card stud one evening at The Mirage in Las Vegas, on fourth street -- after the fourth card was dealt -- I held four diamonds, two down and two up; and, there was only one other diamond that had fallen in the opponents' upcards. With three cards yet to be dealt, I had a good chance of getting a flush -- five diamonds! And that is a very good hand; it will win the pot most of the time. The next two cards dealt to me failed to fill my flush. On the last card, often called the "river," again I was dealt a non-diamond; so my hand was a "failure." It was a "busted flush" in poker terminology.

The player next to me took the pot with a full house, jacks-full. He had three jacks and two fives. On the last card, he had been dealt the jack of diamonds. Think about it: The thickness of a single playing card made the difference as to who would win that hand -- and it was a good-sized pot! The element of luck. . .

In addition, there are various pre-planned steps to help you best play certain combinations of cards under specified conditions; these are the Poker Strategies. These

3

strategies will help you to (1) win more often -- perhaps 75 percent of the time, possibly even more; and (2) win more money ($) when you do win. That is, the Poker Strategies will serve to enhance your chances of winning and optimize the amount of dollars won. Additionally, understanding and properly using the Poker Strategies will make the game of poker all the more exciting and enjoyable for you.

Luck is when preparedness meets opportunity.
-- Ancient Chinese proverb

* * *

Essential Characteristics of a Winner

In a sense, we can regard playing poker as an investment similar to real estate or the stock market or any other form of endeavor or activity where you apply money, time or any other asset in the hope of realizing some goal, such as earning more money.

We can draw an analogy between playing the game of poker and investing in real estate. You are investing both time and money; and, of course, you want to make the most prudent decisions to ensure success. In the real estate investment "game," there is an old adage that says there are three factors essential for success:

Location; Location; Location!

4

This refers to the location of the real estate property that you are considering as an investment. A real estate investment can be profitable only if the location of the property is desirable.

In the case of poker, there are likewise three factors essential to success:

Patience; Patience; Patience!

Success in "investing" in the game of poker requires the utmost of patience -- as you will discern as you read this book. To play by our Basic Poker Rules, and to do so religiously, requires that you be prepared to sit out many, many more hands than you play! A really good poker player -- a *PokerShark* -- may play as few as one out of seven or eight (possibly fewer on some occasions) of the hands dealt to him. *(Note: Throughout this book, we use the masculine gender simply as a convenience. The comments apply equally to both men and women.)*

Without patience, you will play too many hands that are poor investments; and, when you do, it becomes very difficult to be a steady winner. Indeed, you will find that if you are impatient, you are bound to end up a loser -- just as if you invested in real estate in a bad location. This does not mean that patience is the only criterion, but it is essential if you desire to be a winner at the game of poker.

Patience is an essential attribute for winning at poker.

Those of you with an engineering or science background will also recognize that "engineering judgment" can play an important role in the game of poker -- just as it does in many other pursuits. Some call it plain old common sense or "horse sense." You don't have to be an engineer or scientist to use common sense. While you are playing a hand of poker, think about what is going on around you at the table, what cards have fallen, how the other players -- your opponents -- are prone to play their hands, how "strong" each is in his style of play, etc. -- any bit of information that may be available. Factor that information into your thinking and make your decisions accordingly. *Remember that the human brain is a computer; feed the appropriate information into it, process the data, and draw conclusions that lead to successful decisions. Win!*

Carrying our analogy with investments one step further, using good judgment in poker is no different than if you were to make an investment in the stock market: You need to consider all the available data and pertinent factors when selecting the stock in which you plan to invest your money.

An expert poker player might also be likened to a medical doctor or other professional. The M.D. is always "practicing" his profession: The more he practices, the more experience he gains and the more competent he is likely to be. The more knowledge and education he possesses, the better his chances of being an excellent doctor. Similarly, a good poker player will continuously learn from his experiences, by reading this and other books and articles written by experts, and by carefully observing the play of others. It is a truism that practice makes perfect -- but only if you think about the situation and occurrence, draw pertinent conclusions therefrom, and then act accordingly.

After a session of poker, it is good policy to review in your mind some of the more outstanding hands you played, or even some that you observed while sitting out a hand. Sometimes it helps to "think out loud." A good friend or family member can serve as a wonderful "sounding board" to examine the play. Review the situation; ask yourself, What happened; why; how? Try to really understand it. Try to understand the "lesson learned."

A really good poker player -- a winning poker player -- a winner! -- will continuously strive for improvement, aiming at perfection. This is a *PokerShark*!

During the early 1990s, the concept of continuous improvement became known as Total Quality Management, TQM, and was advocated by many government agencies and major corporations as the approach for improving effectiveness -- and achieving success. Likewise, to achieve success in the game of poker or in your life, it is axiomatic that continuous improvement is important in whatever activities you choose to direct or invest your energies or other assets.

As you play the game of poker, think about what you are doing, and how you are doing it. Is it most likely to give you the result you desire? What might you do -- or say -- to increase the size of your winning pot?

Learn from your mistakes too. Everyone makes a mistake now and then. That is part of being "only human."

Carefully analyze your failures and your mistakes; what went wrong and why? Don't just shrug your shoulders and forget about it. Experience is a great teacher, but only if we understand and apply the lessons learned.

We must learn from our mistakes. Otherwise, it has been said, we are doomed to repeat our errors -- and failures. *

Another effective way to improve your poker playing is to watch other players during a game -- especially an expert. Observe his calm, quiet demeanor and patience. He appears relaxed throughout the game. Notice how the expert studies the opponents' upcards. Especially note how few hands he plays from the start; and, for those hands the expert does stay in after the first three cards are dealt -- after the first two cards in Texas hold'em, note how frequently he folds after the next card is dealt.

---

* To prevent recurrence of significant anomalies and failures, the U.S. Air Force Space and Missile Systems Center established a problem prevention program which included various "strategies" describing selected anomalies/failures that had occurred, with suggestions as to how to avoid these. Undoubtedly, this program precluded numerous problems over the years; however, periodically there were failures – usually quite costly ones. In those cases, the contractor either did not have the information provided in the strategy or did not really understand it well enough to properly implement a suitable failure-prevention design and manufacturing process. That was unfortunate. . .

8

Note also that the expert poker player wins a large percentage of the hands he plays to the end. Do not judge an expert by the number of chips in front of him. An expert will maintain sufficient chips so he can build a big pot when holding what is likely to be the winning hand, so as not to have to go "all-in." However, there may be periods when his stack dwindles.

Nor does it follow that a very aggressive player is an expert. An aggressive player is one who frequently bets and raises -- and may often reraise. Playing in games with such players requires further consideration and will be discussed in some detail later in this book. An aggressive player may or may not be an expert. *Controlled* aggressive playing can be an effective strategy.

As part of the Basic Poker Rules for winning at poker, we will discuss how to determine who are the expert poker players at your table -- the PokerSharks -- and who are the PokerPigeons. Understanding this concept is very important in becoming a winning poker player. By learning the Basic Poker Rules and Poker Strategies, you are on your way to becoming a PokerShark. That should be your goal. Once you do so, you will not only win more often and more money, but you will also gain more enjoyment and satisfaction from playing the game of poker. *And, if you think about it, you may be sufficiently astute to apply these Basic Poker Rules and the concept of strategies to achieving greater success in your life.*

* * *

What Are the Special Characteristics of a Winning Poker Player?

A winning poker player -- like a winner in life -- must possess certain key characteristics. Everyone wants to be a winner, but not all achieve this goal.

What are the special qualities or characteristics that make the difference? In the game of poker, everyone can't be a winner -- especially if the house takes a rake out of every pot. It takes time and effort to become a winner. Darwin's Theory of Evolution taught us that the fittest will survive -- and be the winners!

A feature article in the *New Yorker Magazine* summarized the game of poker:

> *"Poker is a game of many skills: You need card sense, psychological insight, a good memory, controlled aggression, enough mathematical know-how to work out the odds as each hand develops, and what poker players call a leather ass -- i.e., patience. Above all, you need the arcane skill called money management: the ability to control your bankroll and understand the long-term implications of each bet (how to avoid the casual five-dollar call that ends in a five-hundred-dollar disaster), so that you don't go broke during a session. . . .*
> *"The pros have lost their sense of urgency . . . . Amateurs . . . want to cram as much action as they*

10

can into the limited time at their disposal, so they stay too long at the table and play until they can't think straight. In order to survive in Vegas, you must divest yourself of the sense of urgency." *

As you read this book, you will learn to understand the implications of this quote, much of which is entwined in the Basic Poker Rules for winning at the game of poker.

PokerSharks Versus PokerPigeons; and Tortoises Versus Hares

The terms "PokerPigeon" and "PokerShark" are intended as metaphors to depict essential differences in the characteristics of losers (the Pigeons) and winners (the Sharks). Certainly, in playing poker, you want to be a Shark rather than a Pigeon, but it is also desirable to be the proverbial Tortoise rather than the fleet Hare. Poker -- like life -- is not a short dash to the finish; it is more like a long marathon race. It requires dedication and perseverance -- and lots of patience.

In Aesop's fable, the Tortoise, despite its slow gait, maintains a steady consistent race (game) to the best of its ability. The Tortoise watches, observes, learns how its opponent plays the game, and how it can best perform to achieve its goal -- and it sticks to this goal to reach the end of the race as quickly as possible. Meanwhile the "swift"

---

* Reference: "The Sporting Scene: No Limit" by A. S. Alvarez; *The New Yorker Magazine*; Vol. LXX, No. 24; August 8, 1994; pp. 56-63.

Hare is over-confident and takes a casual attitude, relaxes along the way, and is generally careless. The Hare does not keep its eye on the goal. In poker, of course, the goal is to win as often and as much money as possible. At least, that is the best benchmark we have to measure one's success in poker.

Like the PokerShark who is out to "devour" his opponents, the PokerTortoise joins the fray only when he knows he has a reasonable -- better yet, a good -- chance of winning the hand and gaining the rewards: the big pot of money ($$$) on the poker table. He plays for the BIG hand -- waiting patiently (slow and steady and sure) for the opportunity to arrive (and it will eventually). Meanwhile he carefully avoids squandering his stake on hunches or unlikely hands -- those for which the odds of winning are very poor. The Hare, on the other hand, is too confident and prone to act in haste without due consideration of the circumstances -- like the poker player who is overly aggressive. And he lacks the patience needed to be a real winner. And so, in the long run, when the race is over, the Hare loses to the Tortoise. . .

The tortoise also wins in the game of life:
A tortoise can live more than 130 years!

* * *

Never dive into murky waters -- Anon.

Why Do We Want to be Winning Poker Players?

It goes without saying that anyone who plays poker -- or any other gambling game -- or invests in real estate or the stock market, does so with the hope and anticipation of being successful, i.e., winning! Yes, there is no doubt that winning money, increasing the size of your stake/assets, should be your main goal -- unless you are just playing to pass the time, i.e., strictly for recreation.

But there is also the thrill of winning, the sheer excitement and satisfaction that comes from succeeding in your endeavors. Accept a challenge and make it work for you! Plan a new venture and pursue it relentlessly until you succeed! There is a certain satisfaction that one realizes, over and above the monetary rewards.

Someone once told me that playing well -- abiding by the Basic Poker Rules and using the Poker Strategies properly -- and winning a "big" hand of poker can be likened to a wonderful sexual experience. Indeed, there is the excitement of the pursuit and anticipation. . . the thrill and exhilaration of the ultimate achievement, sometimes referred to as the climax! And there is a sheer, almost indescribable pleasure that one enjoys.

* * *

On being a better listener --
God gave us one mouth and two ears. Maybe we should take a hint from this and listen more. -- Ed Levenstein, philosopher

Playing Seven-Card Stud

In this section, we will describe the game of seven-card stud. We will also explain many of the terms that are unique to the game of poker. (Later in this book, a full chapter will be devoted to the game of Texas hold'em.) In the following section, we will also explain how the hands are ranked, which applies to all games of poker where the highest hand wins the pot.

There are many games of poker -- perhaps hundreds. There are games such as five-card draw poker, five-card and seven-card stud poker, Texas hold'em, razz, Crazy Pineapple, Omaha, Mexican Poker, Caribbean Stud Poker, etc., etc. In some variations, the lowest hand wins the pot or it may split the pot with the highest hand.

There are many similarities among these games; but there are also significant differences. Each game of poker has its unique character, and the strategies for each will be somewhat different.

As will be explained in the discussion of the Basic Poker Rules, I advocate becoming an expert in just one game of poker -- and strongly suggest that game be seven-card stud, high. Other poker players may prefer a different game. In any case, it is advisable to become expert at one game of poker rather than several. It is difficult enough to become expert in one game without dividing your attention and energies on other games at the same time. Concentrate on being the best you can in one game of poker, and you are bound to be better off than if you spread your mental capacity and time devoted to learning over two or more different games.

Therefore, our emphasis in the first part of this book will be on seven-card stud. The Basic Poker Rules and many of the Poker Strategies, in general, can be applied to any game of poker -- with modifications.

The rules and strategies for Texas hold'em will be discussed in Chapter 5.

• The Stakes

Seven-card stud high is played in almost all poker casinos and is referred to simply as seven-card stud; other games also may be played in casinos depending on the desires of its clientele. In recent years, the game of poker called Texas hold'em has gained considerable popularity. In seven-card stud and other games of poker, the stakes may vary from as low as $1-$2 (often lower in home games) to as high as $200-$400, and possibly higher -- perhaps up to $5,000-$10,000 (in private games).

For example, in a $1-to-$5 game as commonly played in Las Vegas, the minimum bet is $1.00, and the maximum bet is $5.00. This is referred to as a "spread-limit" game. The specified limits set the minimum and maximum bets allowed in that game. A player may make a bet of any amount within these limits. Raises likewise must be within these limits, except the raise must be at least as much as the original bet, but it can be more -- up to the maximum limit.*

In "structured-limit" poker games, as played in many casinos throughout the United States, the house's regulations control the size of the bets and raises. For example, in a typical $2-$4 structured-limit game, the opening bet (or "bring-in") may be specified as a minimum of $1.00 and a maximum of $2.00; the low card on the board must make the opening bet. A raise on the opening round must be equal to the opening bet. On fourth street -- after dealing the fourth card -- and thereafter, the high hand on the board declares first. On fourth street, the amount of the bet is $2.00 unless there is a pair on the board, in which case, a $4.00 bet is permitted. All subsequent bets -- fifth street through seventh street -- are $4.00 with comparable raises. Of course, a player may always check unless another player has already made a bet.

---

* "Betting Structures and Limits" by Donna Harris, Mason Malmuth, and Dan Paymar; *Poker Digest*; May 20, 1999; page 12.

• <u>Five Cards Determine the Winning Hand</u>

The final betting occurs following the dealing of the seventh -- sometimes called the "river" -- card to all players who are still in the hand, i.e., have not "folded" their cards. In seven-card stud, the pot is won by the player showing the highest ranking five-card hand when the cards are turned face up after the final round of betting.

<u>Note</u>: Once a player's cards are turned face down and pushed into the discards -- commonly referred to as the "muck" -- the hand is considered "dead" and is no longer in play.

Although a total of seven cards are dealt to each player, only five of these are used to determine the value of the hand.

• <u>Antes</u>

Depending on where you are playing, there may or may not be an ante -- money placed into the pot by each player before the cards are dealt. Las Vegas is a great place to play lower limit seven-card stud because there is no ante; and also, as will be explained when I discuss the four Basic Rules, there are lots of PokerPigeons there. Casinos in many Indian reservations also have no-ante games. (Of course, you may find PokerPigeons in most other poker rooms. The great attractions for tourists offered by Las Vegas are more likely to provide a number of PokerPigeons at your table.)

• The Poker Table

In seven-card stud, there are usually eight players for a full table, although a few poker rooms use seven hands for a full table. The game may be played with fewer than a full table, but four players is generally the least. The "house" (i.e., the cardroom) is responsible for dealing, monitoring and controlling the game at all times, and resolving any disputes that may arise.

As for the table itself, any shape may do. Generally poker casinos use felt-covered, oval-shaped tables. The dealer, who is an employee of the casino, is seated at the center on one side. The players are identified by seat numbers starting with seat No. 1 through seat No. 8, counting clockwise from the dealer's left.

In home games, any kitchen table will do. Special octagon-shaped tables are often used to accommodate up to eight people. Of course, the players usually know each other by name. In most home games, the players take turns dealing the hands, with the dealer being the last one to receive cards.

• The Deal

During the play, each player still in the hand at the end will be dealt a total of seven cards -- thus the name "seven-card stud." But, as noted above, only five of the seven cards are used to determine the value of the hand and hence the winning hand, based on the rankings.

To start the hand in seven-card stud, each player is dealt two downcards and one upcard. The downcards often are referred to as the cards in the "hole." The upcards are the cards dealt face up. The "board" consists of all exposed cards. (See Chapter 5 for details related to Texas hold'em.)

Then the betting begins. Usually the player with the lowest value upcard must bet first and is required to make at least the minimum bet to open the round. If two or more players show the same value card, then the suit determines the lowest upcard, with ♣ being the lowest, followed by ♦, ♥, and finally ♠ in increasing rank. (Note: The suits are ranked in alphabetical order: clubs, diamonds, hearts, spades.) Thus a 2♣ is lower than a 2♥, which is lower than a 2♠. This is called a "forced" bet. Other criteria for the opening bet may apply in some poker rooms or in home games; for example, the player with the highest upcard may be designated as the first to bet.

After the opening bet, the other players in turn, moving clockwise from the opening bettor, must declare or act in one of the following ways:

- Call -- match the previous bet;
- Raise -- bet at least double the previous bet; or
- Drop out -- often called "fold."

A player signifies that he is folding by turning his cards face down on the table and pushing them toward the dealer. Never expose your hole cards. The dealer will pull your discards face down into the muck, which makes those cards "dead," i.e., no longer in play.

Players are required to act in turn, starting from the left of the bettor. Once a player has checked, if another player has made a bet or raised, the first player must call or raise to stay in the hand when the betting comes around to him again.

In seven-card stud, the fourth, fifth and sixth cards also are dealt face up. In poker parlance, these are sometimes referred to as fourth street, fifth street, and sixth street, respectively. The last (seventh) card is dealt face down, and often is referred to as seventh street or "the river card." There is a round of betting after each card is dealt.

In most poker rooms, the dealer will "burn" the top card before dealing each round by placing that card face down in front of him, keeping those cards separate from the muck or discards.

Starting with fourth street, the "high" hand -- the player showing the highest value upcards -- is first to declare by either betting or checking. Then in clockwise sequence, the remaining players must respond or declare in order. If the high hand has checked, each player in turn is given an opportunity to check or bet. As before, after one player has made a bet, the remaining players in clockwise sequence must call the bet, raise, or fold their cards.

In games with eight players, since there are just 52 cards in a deck, occasionally it will happen that the dealer does not have enough cards to complete the last round. In such a case, the dealer will deal all but the very last card which he will combine with the "burn" cards, mixing them together (ignoring and never using the discards). After cutting these, the dealer will then burn the top card, and deal from the remainder. If there are not enough of these cards to deal one to each player still in the hand, then, after burning the top card, the dealer will turn a "common" card face up. This card represents the seventh and last card for every player in the hand. The dealer will announce this before exposing the common card.

• Cautions

There are a number of house regulations that should be fully understood to avoid making a costly mistake. The following are common examples.

• Although "string" bets or raises are not allowed in many casinos, they occur quite often. This is a raised bet made in more than a single motion or hand movement unless the bettor declares beforehand -- or simultaneously -- that he is betting a certain amount or raising the previous bet. In a typical string bet, the bettor will place some chips in front of the pot and then go back to his stack to take additional chips; this is not permitted. In such a case, the dealer will declare that only the call bet is allowed and return the rest of the chips to that bettor. Thus if you intend to raise, before putting any money (chips) into the pot, it is prudent

21

to simply state, "I raise." Then you may place the money into the pot in more than one hand motion. The same procedure applies to reraises.

• If a player picks up his upcards without calling a bet, and by so doing causes an opponent behind him to act by calling, raising, folding, or exposing his cards, then that player's hand is considered to be "dead" and out of play. This house regulation would not apply (the hand would not be "dead") in a check-check situation (where both players checked) or a bet-and-call situation (where the player in question called a previous player's bet).

• A player must have seven cards -- no more, no less -- to win at the showdown when all cards must be shown at the end of the hand. If the final bet or check is called, the winning player must show all seven of his cards face up.

• All cards must be in full view at all times and must not leave the table except when the hole cards are being viewed.

• Hole cards should not be exposed to any player until the final betting has been completed.

• If a player who is in the pot at the end, having called the final bet or check, turns over his cards to show them, then the "cards speak;" i.e., the dealer will determine the value of the hand, regardless of what the player announces. It is possible for a player to misread his cards. Thus it is prudent to show your cards at the end even if you think you are beaten by another player.

I once observed a player announce in disgust that he had two pair as his opponent showed three-of-a-kind. Fortunately for him, he turned his hole cards face up, showing his hand as he made the announcement. Unbeknownst to him, he had caught a flush. He probably missed seeing it because he was focusing on the two pair and hoping to make a full house. The dealer surprised him by declaring his hand the winner.

In many poker rooms, a player sitting at the table can request to see the cards of another player if the bet (or check) has been called. The dealer will respond by touching these cards to the discards (the "muck"), thus "killing" the cards and rendering them "dead' and out of play. Then the dealer will turn the cards face up for all to see.

However, a special case is when it is the apparent winning player who asks to see the hand of an opponent who has turned his cards face down while saying, "You beat me," or words to that effect. In such a case, if the active player/apparent winner asks to see the other player's hand, the cards remain "alive." The dealer would turn them face up without "killing" the hand by touching them to the muck -- and, if it should turn out that the opponent's cards actually were higher in value, then the dealer would award the pot to the opponent. Thus, if the dealer has declared you the winner, it is prudent not to request to see an opponent's hand. Just sit there and smile as the dealer pushes the chips in your direction.

Someone once said: "Curiosity killed the cat."

- Betting and Raising; Going All In

The amount of the bet and any subsequent raises are predetermined based on the house's regulations for that game. *(Often the dealer will explain the key house regulations when a new player enters the game. If he does not offer, you should not be embarrassed to ask the dealer to do so.)* For example, in a $1-to-$5 spread-limit game in Las Vegas, the opening bet must be at least $1.00; it can be up to $5.00. Subsequent bets or raises cannot exceed $5.00.

There is usually a limit on the number of raises allowed if there are three or more players still in the hand, i.e., that have not folded their cards. (Usually three raises is the maximum allowed.) However, if there are just two players remaining in the hand, then there is no limit on the number of raises permitted. This procedure is designed to avoid a situation where a third player is caught between two -- possibly conspiring -- players who keep raising the pot when one of them has a "sure-fire" winning hand.

Note: In poker parlance, the best possible hand is called the "nuts," meaning there is no way that particular hand can lose the pot. A "monster" hand is a very high one which is not necessarily the "nuts." *I once was in a hand where I held four queens against a player with four nines; another had aces-full, and a fourth had fours-full. They were all monster hands, but only one took the pot. (Fortunately it was mine!)*

During the play of a hand, if a player runs out of money (chips on the table, in front of him), that player is declared to be "all in." That player retains a chance and the right to win the pot to which he has contributed, remaining

24

in the game and continuing to receive cards, but cannot participate in subsequent betting activity; nor can he take any money out of his pocket until that hand is over.

If the all-in player has the highest-value cards at the end of that hand, he can win only the portion of the pot that had been built up until he ran out of money and went all in, i.e., the main pot. The other players are eligible to win the rest of the money -- called the "side pot." Sometimes the side pot is much larger than the main pot. And there may be more than one side pot, depending on the number of players who go all in during the hand.

• Variations Among Poker Casinos

All poker casinos are not alike in their regulations. Some examples where there are significant differences are described below. These can affect how you play the game.

• While most casinos regard eight players as a full table, there are many that have just seven players.

• One poker room in a casino in Lake Tahoe, Nevada, requires the winner of the previous hand to make the opening bet. Other casinos in Lake Tahoe require the player with the lowest upcard to open -- by far the most common practice. However, at this particular casino the minimum opening bet is just $0.50 -- rather than $1.00 -- in a $1-to-$4 spread-limit game.

• "Jackpots" are used in some poker rooms as a means to instill some added excitement into the game. This is a progressive bonus or prize awarded to a player who loses with a monster hand such as aces-full or four-of-a-kind or higher. A small portion of each pot is withdrawn from the table by the dealer and used to build up the size of the jackpot. Usually, the player with the losing monster hand will receive most of the jackpot; the rest is divided between the player who won the pot and the other players seated at the table at that time. Frequently, these are referred to as "bad-beat jackpots."

Some cardrooms offer a prize simply for holding a monster hand; you don't have to lose to win the bonus. These are more modest in amount, but still a pleasant added bonus when you catch four-of-a-kind or better.

Note: To the extent that money for these bonuses is removed from the pot, it will reduce the size of the pot. For this reason, jackpots are not always favored by good poker players.

• <u>The House's Rake</u>

In no-ante games, during the play of each hand, the dealer withdraws chips from the pot for the house's "rake" -- usually 10 percent of the pot up to a specified maximum amount. At the end of the hand, the dealer removes those chips from the table (usually dropping them into a box under the table). For example, consider a $1-to-$5 spread-limit game -- meaning a player may bet from $1.00 up to

$5.00 at any time. In this case, the maximum bet -- the "limit" -- is $5.00. In such a game, the house may take no more than $5.00 as its rake, provided that amount is 10 percent or less of the money in the pot after the final bet. Thus, in this example, if there were, say, $60 in the pot after the final bet, the house would still take only $5.00 as its rake. In some casinos, the house limits its rake to $4.00 maximum (sometimes less) in the $1-to-$5 stakes game.

In casinos where an ante is required, the house usually takes its rake directly from the antes, before dealing any cards, leaving behind the remainder as part of the pot. For example, in a typical $3-$6 structured-limit game with an ante of $0.50 per player, the rake might be $3.00 for a table with 7 or 8 (full table) players. The rake is reduced if there are six or fewer players in the game. The floorperson or manager can allow the rake to be further reduced below the posted figure if there are only a few players at the table. Often, in such cases, one or more players will request a reduction in the rake before anteing for the deal. In most casinos, the dealer must get permission from the floorperson or manager to do so.

In some poker rooms, especially in higher stakes games, the house charges a nominal fee. Periodically, each player at the table will pay a specified amount to the house for the privilege of playing at that table -- similar to a rental fee. Such poker games are called "time-collection" games. For example, in a $20-$40 game, each player might be charged a fee of $7 each half-hour.

It is necessary, of course, that the house take a rake in order to justify its investment. After all, the house (the casino) provides the facilities and personnel to make the game possible. The casino must pay its employees, maintain the facilities, show a profit for its investors, and, of course, pay taxes.

In a $1-to-$5 game with no ante, the house can "earn" as much as $120-$150 per hour from its rake based on 24-30 hands dealt each hour of play, assuming each pot contains $50 or more. This situation is unlikely unless there are a number of very "loose" players who stay in with marginal hands and aggressive players who are wont to raise to build big pots of $50 or more.

In the other extreme, if it is a "tight" table with players who bet only when they have strong hands, the house's share can drop to about half that amount or less, as fewer players stay in and the pots become smaller.

In a typical $0.50-ante game with stakes of $3-$6 structured-limit, for a full table, the house can expect to "earn" somewhat less. With a maximum rake of $3.00 per hand, the House might "earn" $72 per hour -- based on an average of 24 hands dealt each hour; but the house's take is more certain. (As you might expect, the use of an ante tends to slow down the game, so there are fewer hands actually dealt during a given period of time. Of course, some dealers are faster than others, too, and can deal more hands in a given period of time.)

Whatever you are, be a good one.
-- Abraham Lincoln

28

• Why I Prefer No-Ante Games

Perhaps the most significant aspect of what I would call "Las Vegas-type poker" is the absence of an ante in most poker games. This is a definite advantage for those of us who play by the rules for winning at poker. I would much rather play in a no-ante game -- and no rental fee -- where the house takes its rake out of the pot at the end of the game. In such cases, I don't mind the house taking up to 10 percent of the pot so long as I get the rest -- 90 percent or more. *(Note: On the other hand, the use of an ante does tend to build bigger pots because there is some money in the pot from the very beginning -- but not enough to make it my choice.)*

Most important, in a no-ante game, if I decide to drop out after I see my first three cards, it hasn't cost me any money. On the other hand, in ante-type games, it costs money just to sit at the table and be dealt cards.

Further, in a no-ante game, the house takes no money out of the pot if no one calls the opening bet -- the so-called "bring-in." The forced bettor (low card on the board) gets his money back, and the dealer then prepares to deal the next hand. (This occurs occasionally.) On the other hand, in an ante game, the house may take its rake "off the top," directly from the antes, and keep the rake even if no one calls the opening bet.

* * *

If you must procrastinate, do so now; get it over with. -- Anon.

29

• Why Play Poker

Why does one play the game of poker? If it is solely to win as much money as possible, then higher stakes games would be appropriate. Personally, I think the amount won should not be the main goal; the amount won is a measure of success relative to the game stakes.

Certainly it is not wise to play at stakes higher than those at which you feel comfortable or require an investment of more money than you can afford to lose.

For the most part, we have discussed low-limit games, where the stakes are a maximum of $5.00 or, perhaps, as much as $12.00. There are, of course, higher-stakes games; and there are even games where there is virtually no limit on the size of the bets -- only the amount of money (or chips) on the table in front of the player. This often is referred to as a "no-limit" game. Any size bet or raise is allowed.

In a "pot-limit" game, one may bet as much money as is already in the pot; you can imagine how quickly such a pot can escalate in size. The bettor can bet any amount up to the amount of money already in the pot.

By way of illustration, in a pot-limit game, if there is already $20.00 in the pot, the bettor can bet as much as $20.00. And, if the next player decides to raise, he can bet as much as $40.00 and raise $40.00 more. On the next card dealt, with a total of $120.00 in the pot, the next player could bet as much as $120.00. Such a game can quickly build a pot to huge proportions.

In a no-limit game, a player can bet or raise any amount of money he desires so long as he has that amount on the table. The only limitation is the amount of money (chips) the player has in front of him on the table.

I do not advocate very high-stakes games, nor pot-limit and no-limit games -- unless you hope to make a living by playing poker. Presumably a few people do, but it is not something I would recommend to just anyone. Playing poker to support a family and/or to build one's assets -- perhaps with an eye toward retirement or a college fund for your children -- has to be precarious at best. There are bound to be ups and downs. *I just think there have to be better ways to do it.* See Page 32.

Play poker for the excitement, the challenge, the thrill of winning. And, of course, play poker to win $ -- the more you win, the better. Play at a poker game with stakes at which you feel relatively comfortable. Understand that you can lose; you should be well able to afford the amount of money you invest in the game.

This book is intended primarily for persons who either are beginners at the game and want to learn to be winners, or those who already enjoy the challenge of the game (both seasoned and recreational players) and want the excitement and increased profit that comes from playing a hand properly to a successful conclusion. . .

Win more often and win more $!

* * *

• Yes, You Can Become a Millionaire!

There are two ways for a poker player to make a million -- assuming you didn't inherit it, win the lottery, or a big prize on a TV show. One way, of course, is to play in very high stakes games -- or in pot-limit or no-limit games. You can win a lot of money. But that takes a huge investment. To play in such high stakes games, a player ought to have a bankroll of perhaps a hundred thousand dollars or more. That's your playing capital -- money set aside just for playing poker. It is recommended that you have a bankroll of 200-300 times the maximum bet; so for a $200-$400 game, a bankroll of $80,000 or more would be desirable. Not many poker players can afford that kind of bankroll. And besides, recognize that you could lose it all if you happen to have a bad streak of luck.

Besides, anyone who can afford such a steep poker bankroll undoubtedly already has made his million and perhaps a lot more. For most of us, there has to be -- and, indeed, there is -- a better way. . .

• A Better Way for a Poker Player to Become Wealthy

For most poker players, the path to wealth takes two not-so-simple steps:
 • First, win consistently at stakes
 you can afford to play.
 • Second, invest your winnings in assets
 that will grow in value.

How can you be a consistent winner -- one who wins at least 60 percent of the sessions played -- preferably 70-75 percent of the sessions; and, maximize the amount of winnings during those sessions? A corollary is to minimize the losses during losing sessions. There are two basic elements that are involved in being a consistent winning poker player:

(1) Luck
(2) Skill

Luck -- good or bad -- is just a matter of random happenstance. In the long run, luck will even out -- like a ragged sine wave. There will be many ups and downs: periods of good luck and periods of bad luck -- none of predictable duration. It happens to everyone. You have no control over it. The point here is that all poker players are about equal when it comes to the luck factor. *(It may not seem that way sometimes.)*

A winning poker player -- a PokerShark -- will take advantage of the upswings in the luck variations, and optimize his winnings. And, he will minimize losses during periods of bad luck. A player's ability to do this is what we refer to as "skill."

Since the element of luck will even out over the long run, then the big difference is SKILL. How does one acquire it? Learn and apply the four Basic Rules and the strategies for winning at the game of poker, and you will become a skilled poker player. You will become a consistent winner -- a PokerShark. On the other hand, those who

fail to do so are doomed to be your prey -- PokerPigeons,
Perhaps less than 20 percent of poker players are truly
skilled. The rest are your PokerPigeons who will ultimately
provide the funds you need to be on your way to becoming
a millionaire.

After you become a consistent winner at the game
of poker, the next step is fairly logical:

Don't spend the money you win. Invest it instead.

Select assets -- stocks, bonds, real estate -- that will
yield good returns and/or likely appreciate in value. Consider a professional financial advisor to help you select the
best investments.

It helps to also have an investment strategy. For
example, you may want diversified investments. You may
want to select stocks of companies in industries that are on
steep, positive growth curves. Concentrate on those companies that are well managed as indicated by showing the greatest
consistent growth in value over the last several years.

But if you are a gambler, you may want to select a few
stocks among your portfolio that could hit it big, if. . . .
Should you decide to invest in such a company, be sure that
you also have investments in plenty of other good, solid
companies to ensure growth of your overall portfolio.

If you are already in a fairly high income-tax bracket,
consider tax-free municipal bonds. AAA-rated bonds paying 6
percent interest can be the equivalent of a taxable investment
paying 9 percent per year.

Real estate permits you to leverage a relatively small
capital investment to purchase property worth much more
than you invest, that offers a high growth potential. If your

property appreciates 6 percent per year, in twelve years it will be worth double what you paid for it. Had you made a modest downpayment of 20 percent of the purchase price, your actual profit would be nine times your investment! *(I'll leave it to you to make your own calculation.)*

Let's say you are 25-30 years away from retirement, and you have $10,000 to invest. If you can earn interest or profits at an average of 10 percent per year, compounded annually, at the end of the 25 years your $10,000 investment will have grown to almost $100,000. Do that for five consecutive years, and at the end of 30 years, you will have almost $353,000. Combine that with your equity in your home, stock portfolio, municipal bonds, and appreciated real estate investments, and you likely have assets worth well over one million dollars!

**And it all started when you learned
to be a skilled poker player -- a PokerShark. . .**

Note: Certainly I do not intend to advise you -- or anyone else (other than perhaps my family or friends) -- on investments. I may be a PokerShark, but I am not a financial advisor. I can tell you how to become a consistent poker winner, but I leave investment rules and strategies to others more knowledgeable than I.

* * *

"Winning is always better than losing." -- Irene Epstein

What Beats?

Understanding the rankings of the poker hands is extremely important. What beats what? What is the relative value of the possible hands? Without a clear understanding of these facts a player is at a severe disadvantage. It is not advisable to play any game of poker unless you know what beats what. . .

Anyone who plays cards is familiar with the composition of a standard deck of playing cards: Fifty-two cards consisting of four suits -- clubs (♣), diamonds (♦), hearts (♥), and spades (♠); with thirteen cards in each suit. The ace (A) is the highest ranking card, followed by the king (K), then the queen (Q), the jack (J), and then in descending order the ten (10) through the deuce (2). The ace can also be used as a 1 for a 5-high straight (A, 2, 3. 4, 5), sometimes called a "wheel" or "bicycle" -- the best hand in a lowball poker game.

The value of the hand is determined from the best five cards:

> • If there are no matching cards or combinations, the highest ranking card will be the winner. Thus a player holding an ace-high beats another player who has a king-high. And an A-Q would beat an A-J.

> • The ace-high is outranked (i.e., beaten) by a pair of twos (2s) -- two deuces. The high-

est possible pair is two aces -- 2 As. Next, one rank lower is a pair of kings (2 Ks); then a pair of Qs; and so forth for the other cards.

If two players hold the same pair, then the next highest card determines the winner. Thus A-A-Q-3-2 is better than A-A-J-9-8. The suits do not matter.

• A pair of aces (2 As), the highest ranking pair possible, is beat by two pair. The lowest two-pair hand is threes (sometimes referred to as "treys") and deuces, i.e., a pair of threes (two 3s) and a pair of deuces (two 2s). The highest ranking two-pair hand is aces and kings; i.e., a pair of aces plus a pair of kings. (We may refer to these as "treys-up" and "aces-up," respectively, indicating the highest pair of the two-pair hand.)

If two players hold the same two pair, then the value of the fifth card determines which is the winner. For example, a hand consisting of K-K-J-J-10 is better than one with K-K-J-J-9, regardless of the suits. If both players should hold identical value hands, the dealer would split the pot, dividing the pot evenly between the two players.

• Three-of-a-kind -- three cards of the same value -- beats two pair. Thus, three deuces would outrank any two-pair hand.

The best (highest) three-of-a-kind hand is three aces (3 As). Three-of-a-kind is often called "trips" or a "set." Trip aces (3 As) is a great hand to hold and is very likely to be a winner, but it can be beaten. . .

• A straight is next up in the rankings: five cards in sequence. The lowest possible straight is A-2-3-4-5. It is important to note that, in straights, the ace may be used either as the lowest or the highest card. The highest ranking straight is A-K-Q-J-10. A small straight will beat any three-of-a-kind.

If two players both hold straights, then the higher ranking straight takes the pot. The suits do not matter. If both straights are identical, the two players will split the pot. (This is a rare occurrence.)

• A flush -- five cards of the same suit -- beats a straight. The highest card in the flush determines who wins if two or more players hold flushes. Thus a flush with an ace -- an A-high flush -- beats a K-high flush. The suit does not matter.

If two players have ace-high flushes, then the next highest card determines the winner. Accordingly, an A-K-Q-9-2 flush would beat an A-K-J-10-9 flush, regardless of the suits. And an A-K-Q-9-2 flush would beat an A-K-Q-8-7 flush.

• Next in the sequence of rankings is a full house -- three-of-a-kind plus a pair in the same hand. The highest possible full house is three As and two Ks. This is called "aces full of kings." The lowest ranking full house is three 2s and two 3s, called "deuces full of treys."

• Four-of-a-kind (also called "quads") is a really super hand! In fact, it's a "monster" hand. When you catch one on the river -- or, better yet, on an earlier round -- wow! Your excitement will be hard to control. The highest possible four-of-a-kind hand you could hope to get is four aces; but even four 2s is almost certain to be a winning hand. But be aware that there may be times when two players catch four-of-a-kind.* Of course, only the player with the highest ranking card will take the pot. Four jacks is better than four 10s. When a player loses such a hand, he may have experienced "a bad beat," if he loses to a long-shot draw or highly improbable hand.

---

* I've seen it happen several times. Once I held four nines against a player with four sixes. We raised each other until he ran out of money!

• To beat four-of-a-kind, a player would need to hold a higher four-of-a-kind or a straight flush: five cards in sequence, all of the same suit. For example, 7-8-9-10-J, all of one suit, would beat four aces. Can you imagine being in a hand when you catch a straight flush against a player with four-of-a-kind or a full house!

• Finally, the best possible hand in seven-card stud poker -- or any other high poker game -- is a royal straight flush (sometimes simply called a "royal" or a "royal flush"): A-K-Q-J-10, all in the same suit. These hands are extremely rare. You may never have one dealt to you. In some poker rooms, the suit may serve to further define the rank: spades higher than hearts, which is higher than diamonds; and clubs is the lowest ranking suit.

It is important that a player fully understand the rankings and relative value of the hands in poker. Memorize these if at all possible so you don't have to spend time thinking about the sequence; know it. There are enough other things to consider during the play of a hand, that it is best not to have to stop to ask yourself about the relative value or ranking of the various possible hands.

Sometimes new players are confused as to the ranking of a straight versus a flush versus a full house. It is recommended that you clearly understand the differences before you sit down to play for money.

For new players, some poker casinos will provide a small, handy card showing these rankings.

When my daughter first started playing poker, she had not played poker in her growing-up days and felt unsure about the rankings. So she kept such a card at the table beside her stack of chips; it helped her to remember the rankings and gave her some degree of confidence. However, it also told the opponents at her table that she was a novice at the game, and some tried to take advantage of that fact. They were soon to learn that she was a PokerShark, a Tortoise, and a consistent winner. She has an incredible win record. That's because she religiously follows the Basic Poker Rules for winning at poker.

To summarize, following is a flow chart showing the rankings of hands starting with no pair and finally reaching the royal straight flush, the best possible hand a player could hope to hold. In using such a chart, keep in mind that the higher the cards in each category, the greater the value of the hand. Thus an ace-high straight is better than a 10-high straight, and a flush with a king and queen beats one with a king and jack. Three kings beats three queens if both players hold three-of-a-kind; and two-pair, aces-up, beats two-pair, jacks-up. Of course, even three deuces will beat aces-up. If no one has a pair -- it does happen -- then the highest card wins; an ace-high would beat a king-high. If two players have ace-high, then the next highest ranking card determines the winner; accordingly an ace-queen beats an ace-jack. The suits do not matter in such cases.

No Pair
↓
Pair
↓
Two Pair
↓
Three-of-a-Kind
↓
Straight
↓
Flush
↓
Full House
↓
Four-of-a-Kind
↓
Straight Flush
↓
Royal Straight Flush

It's fun to win!

Poker Room Regulations

Most poker rooms or casinos have house rules or regulations regarding the playing of poker on their premises. These include restrictions on smoking and other things that may be annoyances. You should become familiar with these regulations before playing there. Before entering a game, it is wise to ask about these regulations if you are not sure. Some of these regulations usually are posted on the wall for all to see.

• Of particular importance are the regulations on raising. Checking and raising usually is permitted. Thus, suppose you are high on the table and believe you are holding the best hand. There is another player who has been betting and you believe he is likely to continue to do so. You might check and wait for him to bet; hopefully others will call. Then, when it is your turn to respond, you can make a raise and "earn" at least one additional bet if you win the hand.

In limit poker games, there usually is a limit on the number of raises -- most often three, or perhaps four, raises -- if there are three or more players in the hand at that point. But, with only two players remaining in the hand -- often referred to as playing "heads-up" or "head-to-head"-- there may be no limit on the number of raises permitted. In that case, the only limit is when one of the two players runs out of money.

In most no-limit or pot-limit poker games, there is no limit on the number of raises allowed. Again, the only limit is the amount of money or the number of chips each player has in front of him.

• In most poker rooms, only the money -- or the chips -- on the table at the start of the deal can be played; in no case is a player allowed to "go into his pocket" for more money until after the hand has been completed and a winner declared. (This is normally referred to as "table stakes.") Most poker casinos require that only chips be used in the betting; a few allow cash as well as chips. Usually, chips are not allowed to be removed from the table until a player leaves the game. (The chips may be changed for different denomination chips at any time; but the value may not be changed.)

• If a player goes all in with a bet of less than half of a full bet, a subsequent player who has yet to bet has the option of calling the partial bet, completing the bet to the full amount, or folding. On the other hand, an all-in wager of half a bet or more is treated as if it were a full bet; and, a subsequent player can make a full raise if he so desires.

• As an alternative or in addition to announcing that he is checking, a player may simply tap or knock on the table with his hand or finger. (If a player does this accidentally when it is his turn to declare, it is regarded as a check. *Be careful of your hand movements*.)

• Acting out of turn -- before the betting gets around to you -- is not permitted. If you are not ready to declare your bet or check when the betting comes around to you, it is appropriate to call "time" at that point.

Many players and dealers become annoyed with an unduly long delay, so it should be avoided if possible. However, if you need to think out the playing of the hand or contemplate the chance of catching the card you need to make your hand, don't be pressured into making a snap decision that could be very costly. Take the time to examine the cards on the table, consider the odds, whatever is needed to make your decision. After all, you are considering making an investment. But be reasonable so as not to cause undue delay in the game.

If you do not stop the action by calling "time," and three or more players act after you (bet, check or fold), you may lose your right to act. However, if a player before you has yet to act, you will not forfeit your right to act even if three players behind you do so while you are waiting.

• In limit poker games, if a player makes a motion with his chips indicating a bet, and thereby induces another player to act, he is required to complete that action.

• If a player puts a single chip into the pot that is larger in value than the amount of the previous bet, and does not declare "raise," he is presumed to have simply called the bet. For example, if the previous player had bet $4.00 and the next player threw a $20 chip into the pot without any comment, the second player has only called the $4.00 bet. The dealer will give him change in chips to make up the difference.

    • Because it happens quite frequently, it is appropriate that we reiterate the issue of a "string" bet or raise: when a player places money (chips) into the pot in two separate motions without first declaring the amount of the bet or intent to raise. This would also be the case if a player were to state, "I call your bet," placing the money in front of the pot, and then added, "and I raise you $4.00," placing the additional money in front of the pot. The dealer would only allow the call bet and would return the second $4.00 to the player. If the bettor had declared, "I raise you $4.00," or simply said "raise" <u>before</u> putting any money into the pot, there would be no problem. Be aware of this common house regulation so you won't make the mistake. On a string bet or raise, only the call bet is allowed.

    However, if a bettor places chips in front of the pot that total one and a half or more times the previous bet, he is regarded as having raised the bet. In such a case, the bettor is required to add the additional chip(s) to complete the raise. *(Sometimes a player will feign a raise by holding a large stack of chips in his hand while making the bet, but releases only the amount needed to call the previous bet. This is a legal maneuver, though not one we would recommend.)*

    • When making a bet or raise, the money or chips should be placed in front of you and in front of the pot -- not directly into the pot. This permits the dealer to verify that the proper amount has been bet/raised by you. After all players have made their bets, the dealer will push all of the bets into the pot in the center of the table before dealing the next card -- or, if it is seventh street, asking the players to show their hands.

• The last player to bet or raise is expected to show his cards first; the others (those who called that bet) follow in clockwise order *(but this protocol is not always followed)*.

• Protecting your cards: Each player is responsible for protecting his own hand at all times.* Otherwise the hand may be declared "dead" if it is fouled by another player's action or the dealer accidentally "kills" the hand by mingling cards with the muck.

---

* I was in a hand of $2-$4 seven-card stud, holding what I believed would be the winning hand. On sixth street, a player to my left who had sat down at the table just a few hands earlier, suddenly folded his hand, throwing his cards on top of mine instead of into the muck. As he started to retrieve his cards, he also placed his hand on top of some of my cards. I held onto my cards with all my might, protecting them with one hand, while separating his cards from mine with the other hand. It may have been an accident -- or it might have been a deliberate attempt to foul my hand. *(I'll never know.)* By protecting my hand, I was able to win a big pot.

• For each game, the casino has an established minimum "buy-in;" i.e., the minimum amount of money a "new" player entering the game must invest in the purchase of chips. A full buy-in usually is five times the maximum bet for that game. Thus, in $2-$4 seven-card stud, the minimum buy-in is $20.00. During the game, many casinos limit a player to one "short" buy-in -- less than the minimum (or "full") buy-in. Once a player goes all in, subsequent purchase of chips requires at least a full buy-in. Sometimes short buy-ins may be alternated with full buy-ins. *(In practice, this regulation is not strictly enforced, depending on the dealer.)*

If a player changes tables voluntarily, he must start at that table with at least a full buy-in. This does not apply if he is transferred to another table because of a "broken" game at the first table -- e.g., too few players. Most poker players do not want to play with less than five players. A PokerShark would hate to waste his time at such a table; his chances of winning any significant amount of money would be severely reduced.

• A pot will not be awarded until after all losing hands have been placed into the pile of discards -- the muck. If you show the best hand, make sure that your hand doesn't get "mucked," perhaps by error, until after all of the losing hands. *Always protect your hand!*

• Casino regulations dictate behavior. Profane or abusive language is not allowed, nor are verbal or physical threats, creating a disturbance, or shouting. Throwing the cards or anything else, for that matter, is off limits. Just because the cards don't come your way is no reason to express your anger or disappointment so forcibly. *(Playing poker is more enjoyable for everyone when those involved are pleasant -- win or lose. That applies to players, dealers, floorpersons, and casino staff and management.)*

• Poker is played throughout the world. In the U.S., while there may be players representing various ethnic origins, most casinos require that only English be spoken at the table. Don't be shy about asking the dealer to intercede if you observe a non-English language spoken at your table in a casino in the U.S.

* * *

*Doing the best at this moment
puts you in the best place
for the next moment.*
                            -- Oprah Winfrey

A Little on Statistics

As a matter of interest, in seven-card stud there are almost 134 million possible combinations or hands that can be dealt from a deck with 52 cards. Statistically, a hand will be dealt without a single pair 17.4 percent of the time. One pair will occur in 43.8 percent of the hands -- by far the most common hand. Two pair will occur 23.5 percent of the time. Three-of-a-kind will be dealt 4.8 percent of the time. A straight will show up in 4.6 percent of the hands dealt. You can expect a flush 3.0 percent of the time; a full house just 2.6 percent; four-of-a-kind, only 0.17 percent; and a straight flush, a mere 0.03 percent.*

From a strictly statistical viewpoint, the mean hand is between a pair of 10s and a pair of jacks; i.e., there is an equal number of higher and of lower ranking hands possible.

Starting with a pair, the higher the ranking, the greater is its value. However, statistically, a pair of deuces will occur just as frequently as a pair of aces or any other pair. Of course, the higher the value of the pair, the more desirable it is. Thus a pair of aces will beat any other pair, although the probability of occurrence is the same.

If you start with a pair, the odds are 1.4-to-1 against making two pair, and 4.1-to-1 against ending up with three-

---

* "Tough Seven-Card Stud Quiz" by Charles Morris; *Poker Digest*, May 20, 1999; pages 8 and 74.

of-a-kind or better. Starting with three-of-a-kind dealt to you, the odds are 1.5-to-1 that you will not make a full house or better.*

To illustrate, if your first three cards include a pair, then the chance of making two pair is about 40 percent; three-of-a-kind will show up less than 10 percent of the time; a full house will occur about 7.5 percent of the time; and you will catch four-of-a-kind about 0.5 percent of the time. More than 36 percent of the time, you can expect to be left with just the original pair; i.e., no improvement.

You don't have to be a mathematician to realize that it is more difficult to be dealt four-of-a-kind than three-of-a-kind. Two pair is much more common and easier to get than three-of-a-kind -- about five times. And you can expect to be dealt one pair almost twice as often as two pair.

---

* "A Course in Seven-Card Stud Poker" by Lynne Loomis and Mason Malmuth; *Poker Digest*; Jan. 14, 1999; pages 18-19.

One Big Difference Between Life and the Game of Poker:
- **In life, you have to accept the hand you are dealt, and play it as best you can.**
- **In poker, you can fold that hand and wait for the next opportunity.**

-- George Epstein

CHAPTER TWO --
THE FOUR BASIC POKER RULES FOR WINNING

It takes PERSONAL DISCIPLINE to be a winner!

The four Basic Poker Rules for Winning are extremely important. They are the basis for being a winner at the game of poker, regardless of the game you choose to play. In fact, these rules can be applied to any gambling game -- and they can be applied to your own life with some modifications in terminology. If you follow these rules carefully, you are bound to be a winner in the long run. Otherwise, you will be a loser, and you can bet on it.

We will summarize the four Basic Poker Rules and then explain each in detail. We will also discuss exceptions.

**Rule #1: Set Your Goal and Limits;
Use Money Management**

— **Winning Goal**
— **Losing Limit**
— **Effective Money Management**

**Rule #2: Carefully Select the Game
and Table at Which You Play**

— **Seven-Card Stud May be Best**
— **PokerSharks vs. PokerPigeons**
   *Don't Play Against Players
   Who Are Better Than You*
— **Table Position**

Rule #3: *Don't Lose!*
   **Play Only Those Hands You Have
   a Good Chance of Winning**

— **Three-of-a-Kind**
— **Three Cards to a Straight**
— **Three Cards to a Flush**
— **Medium to High Pairs**
— **Small Pair with a High "Kicker"**

   The Details and Exceptions

Rule #4: *Be ALERT!*
**Don't Drink Alcoholic Beverages
or Use Drugs While Playing Poker;
Don't Play If You Are Tired or Disturbed**

- **Rule #1:**

SET YOUR GOAL AND LIMITS; USE MONEY MANAGEMENT

When you sit down to play poker, you should have a goal in mind: How much do you hope to win during this session? Your objective certainly is to win, but your goal should be to win a reasonable amount of money. For example, suppose you start the game with a stake of $50; in that case a reasonable goal might be to double your money. Perhaps you have set a higher goal: You will consider quitting when you have won $100 -- or perhaps $200. Whatever you decide, when that goal is reached, the time has come to think about leaving the game until the next session. Many poker players do exactly that: They quit when they reach their goal.

These considerations also may be applied to any other gambling game. For example, if you are playing the slots or roulette, whether in Las Vegas or elsewhere, the odds are set in favor of the house (the casino). *That's the casino's "edge."* If you play long enough, the casino ultimately will be the winner; you will be the loser. However, in the short term, you may be ahead at some particular time. The key to coming away a winner is to quit while you are ahead. *Easier said than done, isn't it. . .*

It's not a bad idea. Get up from the table with your chips, cash them in, and go for a walk -- or enjoy a leisurely meal in the coffee shop. If you are visiting Las Vegas and staying in the hotel, go up to your room for a rest, or take a walk on the Strip to enjoy the scenery. Explore one of the other hotels, or just people watch. There is so much to see in Las Vegas. If it is in the afternoon and the weather is good, perhaps a dip in the pool would be refreshing. Certainly, if you are tired and it is late, then it is long past the time you should have quit the game for the night.

For most of us, it is hard to quit the game when you are winning, especially if you have been playing only a short time. It takes a lot of will-power to get up from the table under those circumstances, although I have seen many good players do just that.

• Money Management

A preferable approach involves money management. You are winning and have surpassed your original goal, you're not tired, and it's a "good" game — so you really don't want to quit playing. Just move one stack of your chips a few inches to the side of the rest of the chips. (Note: A player is not allowed to remove chips from the table while s/he is in the game.) This "side-stack" represents a portion of your winnings. Perhaps it is equal to your original buy-in. Now, mentally consider this your playing stake for the remainder of the session. If you lose that stack, then it is time to quit the game — no ifs, ands, or buts. . . It does take some self-discipline.

Another money management concept when you are winning is to pile your chips into stacks with, say, 30 or 40 chips in each stack. Count the number of stacks. When the number of stacks drops one full stack, it is time to quit the game. If you continue to win and increase the number of stacks, great! But when you lose back one full stack, it's time to leave the game.

• But If You Are Losing...

Of course, there is the element of luck. Certainly there is no guarantee that you will win every time. In fact, it is almost certain that you will lose on occasion if you play poker often enough -- no matter how expert you are. There will be times when you get good hands and play them just right -- only to lose to better hands. Coming in second in poker can be expensive. The rules and strategies for winning at poker will help you avoid and minimize those instances, but it happens to the best of poker players. That's just part of life...

Therefore, along with your winning goal (and money management technique), you should also set some limits:

(1) How much money are you willing to lose at that session?

Be sure that you can readily afford to lose that amount, because you may... For example, perhaps you are willing (if necessary) to lose your entire starting stake. Or, perhaps you are willing to invest in a second or even a third stack of chips if necessary. When you come to the table to play poker, have a firm figure in your mind as to your limit on losing -- the most amount of money you will allow yourself to lose.

I would suggest a limit of five times the minimum buy-in. In a $3-$6 game, that would be:

$$5 \times \$30 = \$150$$

Realize that usually you will not start out a winner at a session of poker; you need sufficient funds available to sustain you until you start to win some hands. If you cannot afford such a loss, you should not be playing at those stakes; go to a smaller limit.

(2) How long a time should you play at that session?

A typical poker session might be four to five hours in length, at most eight hours -- depending on your personal stamina and attention span. It could be a shorter period of time. If you are well rested before you come to the casino, you may be able to play a lot longer than if you had just arrived after a full day of work.

Of course, the longer you sit at the table and play, the more tired you will become -- and the more likely you will be careless and make a costly mistake. And then you are more likely to deviate from the Basic Poker Rules and forget the Poker Strategies. *(Incidentally, if you see a player at the table who is having trouble staying awake -- he keeps nodding off, you can assume that he is a PokerPigeon, and not a PokerShark; indeed, that is the kind of opponent you want to play against.)*

Note that we have suggested that the length of time you play at one session be based entirely on your personal stamina and ability to remain alert. <u>There is no arbitrary time limit</u>. Another consideration: Perhaps the time to quit that session is when you get the feeling that you are bound to lose.

When either of these limits is reached, the prudent poker player will quietly pick up the remaining chips in front of him, smile, and bid a pleasant good-bye to those at the table. They may not pay much attention to his departure; but if he leaves with lots of "their" chips, they will notice and may even comment. *(They would like him to stay so they can win back "their" money.)*

If the cards have been running against you, don't try to "press your luck" to win it all back. There will be many more opportunities to win -- and, so long as you abide by the Basic Poker Rules for winning at poker, you will be a winner in the long run. Remember, tomorrow is another day. . .

* * *

The human brain is a wonderful thing. It starts working the moment you are born, and never stops until you stand up to speak in public. -- George Jessel, comedian

- **Rule #2:**

CAREFULLY SELECT BOTH THE GAME AND TABLE AT WHICH YOU PLAY

Selecting the Game of Poker to Play

If You are Determined to Gamble, It's Best to Play Poker

Casinos offer a wide variety of gambling games including table games and slot machines of almost a limitless variety. Taking advantage of the growing popularity of poker, many casinos have introduced card games -- and even slot machines or video poker -- that resemble poker in many respects. Among the more popular *poker-type* card games is Caribbean Stud. More recently a variation of this game, Bahamas Bonus, was introduced. Pai Gow, Three-Card Poker and Let It Ride are also quite popular in many casinos. In all of these table games, the players compete against the casino -- the house, represented by the dealer.

If you play in any of these games, like all other casino gambling games (slots, roulette, craps, keno, etc.) -- except poker, you are handicapped from the start: The odds are necessarily designed to be in favor of the house.

For example, in Caribbean Stud, the house's advantage is 4.4 percent if you play absolutely perfectly; more often it is between 8 percent and 12 percent. You may be interested to know that slot machines are the big moneymakers for U.S.

casinos. The average casino "earns" about two-thirds of its profits from its slot machines.

While the house's "edge" may be only a few percentage points, the longer you play, the more $ you invest, the more of your $ the house will keep. You may have periods of winning; but, in the long run, the house must be ahead. Generally, the house expects to "keep" about 20 percent of all the money bet in its casino. *(How else can it pay all its expenses and show a profit for the stockholders?)* Even in those games where there may be some skill or judgment involved in playing, in the long run the house must win. *A poker-playing friend of mine once likened playing the slots to "throwing your $ at the machine; what bounces back you get to keep." With the newer, computerized slot machines, you can do it faster than ever.*

Poker is different. Much different. Here you are playing against other players -- not against the house. If you have greater skill than the other players -- your opponents -- you can expect to win more often than not. Of course, the house gets its rake; it deserves it. It just means that you have to win a little more to make up for your share of the rake.

Conclusion: If you want to gamble and win $, poker is your best bet. . .

Optimism is the faith that leads to achievement. Nothing can be done without hope.
-- Helen Keller

Which Game of Poker Should You Play?

Having decided that poker is the best gambling game for you, now the big question is which game of poker should you undertake? In which game of poker should you become an expert? Where would it be most advantageous for you to invest your time, energy, and money?

All games of poker are not equal. There are a wide variety of poker games available, and betting stakes can range from pennies to hundreds -- even thousands -- of dollars. Needless to say, it is important to be comfortable with the game and stakes you play. The stakes should be high enough to be meaningful for you and to permit you to be effective when raising or bluffing -- on carefully selected occasions, of course -- yet not so high that you have "butterflies" in your stomach when you are raised or reraised.

Popular poker games include draw poker, stud poker, low-ball poker, high-low poker, Texas hold'em, Omaha, Mexican Poker, and razz. There are literally dozens, perhaps hundreds, of others -- some with catchy and unlikely names such as such as Spit in the Ocean, Baseball, Monte, Crazy Pineapple, 'Round the World, Crossover, Criss Cross, Twin Beds, Hurricane, Black Maria, and Screw Your Buddy. There are games with wild cards too, where a particular card -- it could be the joker or any deuce, or even one-eyed jacks, for example -- may be used as an ace or as any card you want in straights or flushes.

Considering all these variations, if you really want to be a winner, you should select and play one particular game of poker. It is difficult enough to become expert at one game, never mind two or more. Yes, it is possible to master more than one game of poker, but it would really be stretching your intellectual facilities and time.

Use your assets for your maximum benefit.

You don't have to be a genius to realize that you become more expert in something when you concentrate your efforts. That's why so many professionals are specialists -- doctors, lawyers, engineers, even professional athletes. If you are a baseball player, it is far better to be a great shortstop than to try to excel in several positions at the same time -- although some have been able to do so. I would much rather be a wonderful science teacher than a mediocre one teaching various subjects.

Specialize so you can excel!

So one way to become a consistent winner at the game of poker is to be expert at one particular game -- not all of them. Specialize and know that game like "the palm of your hand." Learn the strategies for that game so it becomes almost second nature for you. And that is a key part of Basic Poker Rule #2.

As for which poker game is the "right one" for you in which to specialize and become expert, that, of course, should be the game at which you are most likely to win --

the game at which you can win most often. That is the poker game which offers you the best chance of winning the most often and the most $ (relative to the stakes) when you play by the other Basic Poker Rules; it is the game that best allows you to apply the Poker Strategies to optimize your performance. In short, it is the particular game of poker that provides you the best chance of winning when you play well and properly. In my opinion, that game is seven-card stud -- played with no wild cards. Indeed, seven-card stud is one of the most popular games played in most poker rooms and casinos throughout the country. *(At this point, you might want to review the discussion in Chapter One on Playing Seven-Card Stud.)* Other skilled poker players have selected other games in which to specialize. In particular, Texas hold'em has become quite popular. Certainly, there are advantages and disadvantages in each case.

Why I Prefer Seven-Card Stud

In seven-card stud, you are provided considerable useful information while each hand is being dealt. Each player will receive four upcards during the hand -- if he doesn't drop out along the way. The board is spread out before you offering lots of useful information. Knowing your hole cards and all of the upcards, of course, places you in a better position to use good poker judgment in deciding how to play a hand. Should you fold? Should you check, bet, or raise? Is this a good spot to pull a bluff? Also, you can watch how the other players, your opponents, react to the upcards as they are dealt out -- both their own and the other players' upcards. From this, you can learn a lot about what they may be holding, as well as how they play the game. Then you are in a better position to use your judgment during that hand and subsequent hands. The more information available to you, the better position you are in to apply the Poker Strategies.

On the other hand, there are skilled poker players who prefer Texas hold'em because they do not have to track the cards that have been dealt and folded. They don't have to remember the upcards that have been folded. It requires less mental effort on their part. In other words, they prefer to play with less — not more — information. *(Another way of looking at this choice is that they forsake the opportunity to use such information to their advantage over their opponents.)*

No Wild Cards

Playing poker without wild cards is also to your advantage when you learn to be a PokerShark. Wild cards make the element of luck an even greater factor than it would be otherwise. A poor player — a PokerPigeon — is more likely to draw a card to beat you if wild cards are available. An expert player -- a PokerShark -- has a better chance of winning by reducing the "luck factor." Don't play poker with wild cards.

Luck favors those who prepare for it.
— Ancient Chinese proverb

Selecting the Table

At this point, you have selected the game and stakes at which you wish to invest your time and money. Now comes a very important decision: There may be several "tables" of seven-card stud or Texas hold'em at the stakes you would like to play -- and, like many other things in life, all tables are not equal. If you want to win, you need to carefully select the table. Basically, you want to play at a table where there is $ going into the pot -- where there is "action;" and you want to play against opponents you can beat.

A good rule of thumb is that you want to play at a table filled with "happy, jocular players who call most bets and seldom raise."* There is a lot of cross-table chitchat and laughter. Some players are drinking alcoholic beverages. Some are intently watching the football game on a big screen on the side of the room while playing their hands or betting on the horse races.

The poker "table" is more than a structure with a flat surface covered with green felt; it is made up of people -- and that is the major factor. Each person is an individual; each plays the game somewhat differently than the others. Some are good players; some are poor players. A few are likely to be very good players -- experts, or what we have referred to as "PokerSharks."

---

* "Bad Game, Good Game" by Lou Krieger; *Card Player*; Nov. 29, 1996; pages 20-21.

Players in poker games in resort areas include many tourists and a significant number of "town people," sometimes referred to as the "regulars" or the "locals." These latter individuals tend to be expert players -- but not always. Some "regulars" think they are experts. As a general rule, you should try to avoid playing at a table with more than one or, at most, two "regulars." Usually the "regulars" are more skilled and very "tight" players. A tight player is one who plays relatively few hands, and seldom bets unless he has a strong hand. You can identify the "regulars" because they know each other on a first-name basis; they may discuss mutual acquaintances; and, often, they are openly friendly with the dealers and other employees in the poker room. Some spend a good deal of the time socializing. Certainly, all "regulars" are not experts; and, furthermore, you will find that some of the tourists may very well be expert poker players -- PokerSharks in fact!

"Recreational" players are people who play for the enjoyment of the game. Sure, they want to win money, but that is not their primary goal. Some of these players may also be PokerSharks, but not likely.

PokerSharks Versus PokerPigeons

If we call the expert players the "PokerSharks," then we might refer to the poorly skilled players as the "PokerPigeons." *(While we have no firm statistics, we might estimate that about 10-20 percent of poker players can be considered to be PokerSharks. The rest are PokerPigeons to some degree.)* What distinguishes these individuals?

At first glance, there are no special or unique characteristics. It is only after you have watched them play and bet that you can discern real differences.

In a broad sense, the PokerPigeons are people who came to play -- as contrasted with the PokerSharks who play to win. This is generally true wherever you play poker; there are PokerSharks and PokerPigeons in every poker room.

Some are bigger PokerPigeons than others by virtue of their more careless style of play. Really "big PokerPigeons" play almost every hand; sometimes they call to the end with a practically impossible hand. (These are very "loose" players. They may or may not be aggressive.) You would be surprised at how many of these there are! For the most part, the PokerPigeons do not use the Basic Poker Rules for winning at poker; nor do they know the Poker Strategies.

Your objective is to win money ($). To do this, you want to learn how to be a PokerShark, and you want to play poker against as many PokerPigeons as possible. That's logical. After all, the more "pigeons" at your table, the better your chance of winning more $. The "bigger" the "pigeons," the more money you are likely to win. So, how can you select a "good" table?

It is really not that difficult. A "good" table is one at which you are likely to win consistently and a considerable amount of money relative to the game stakes. You can win more often and more $ with the winning hand the more PokerPigeons playing at your table. That certainly makes good sense. I don't mean to disregard the "luck" factor; but, in the long run, the PokerPigeons are bound to lose to the PokerSharks. Since you are a better poker player, you are more likely to win more hands from these PokerPigeons.

I once observed a PokerPigeon draw to an inside straight. He held 5-6-8-9 unsuited. He needed a seven to fill the straight. Laying there on the table in the opponents' upcards for all to see were three sevens; there was only one seven possibly left in the deck -- assuming it wasn't in another player's downcards or among the burn cards or discards.

A player with a pair of aces on board was high on sixth street and bet the maximum. Another player called showing a possible flush, as did our PokerPigeon. Would you believe it? His river card was the case seven. He had filled the straight. Talk of luck; talk of long shots -- about 1 chance in 30 -- and he caught it! He took the pot when the flush failed to connect and the pair of aces had two pair. But in the long run, the PokerPigeon is bound to be a big loser in the game of poker.

Furthermore, as you learn and then apply the various Poker Strategies we will describe, the PokerPigeons are more likely to stay in and chase your "made" (generally, winning) hands.

As was noted above, PokerPigeons are the opponents who <u>came to play</u>; they are, in the extreme case, players who would draw to an inside straight -- and do so even after most, if not all, of the cards they need have fallen in their opponents' upcards. They are the ones who pay and pay, continuing to call bet after bet, when holding three to a flush even if most of their needed suit cards have already been exposed in the other players' upcards. A PokerPigeon is likely to be a person who came to the table with $100 in a $1-to-$5 game, and sits there calling and calling, perhaps even raising, hand after hand -- until finally he loses his $100. And then the PokerPigeon likely may very well take another $100 bill out of his wallet to buy another stack of chips. After all, he "came to play!"

If a PokerPigeon happens to be seated next to you, that's great -- especially if he is seated to your right so you can raise after he has bet or raised.

A few words about your treatment and attitude toward PokerPigeons:

• Be courteous at all times. It's okay to engage in conversation but don't get too friendly. You certainly don't want him to resent it when you raise and win a big pot; nor do you want to feel obligated to just call when you really should raise. It's best that the PokerPigeon enjoys playing -- and losing to you; so be pleasant and cheerful.

• In no case should you lecture him on the poor play he made. For one thing, he might resent it. Further, why would you want to help him to become a better poker player? It's to your advantage to play against as many PokerPigeons as possible; the bigger the "pigeon," the better.

Very important --

If a player goes in almost every hand, he is unquestionably a PokerPigeon -- especially if he continues to stay in almost every hand after the fourth card is dealt. No one can consistently have that kind of good luck.

On the other hand, a PokerShark plays relatively few hands -- on average, perhaps only one out of seven or so hands. Usually, he will sit at the table and throw in his cards hand after hand, waiting for a hand worthy of the investment. (He has lots of patience.) The PokerShark wins a significant fraction of the hands in which he invests an opening bet, i.e., calls or bets on third street. And the PokerShark will win even a higher portion of the hands he stays in beyond the fourth card -- fourth street.

Some PokerSharks prefer to be seated at the table in seat No. 1, immediately to the left of the dealer, in the so-called "first position." *(The reason for this will be explained later when we discuss table position.)*

More often than not, a PokerShark will look at his hole cards just once at the start of the hand, and not again until he is considering folding or raising, or perhaps once more before making the final bet on the river. This is good practice so as to minimize the possibility of exposing your hand to others. *(When looking at your hole cards, use your hands to shield them from your neighbors' view while you turn up only the corner next to you. Never lift the cards off the table.)* PokerPigeons are prone to look at their hole cards quite often. *(Look at your hole cards once and remember what they are. But if you are not certain, by all means take another look.)*

PokerSharks concentrate on the game. They carefully observe the game even after they fold. They study the other players' upcards, watching their facial expressions and physical actions. They are busy assessing the cards as they are dealt, and the playing of the hand. PokerPigeons, on the other hand, are likely to be engaged in other extraneous activities -- perhaps flirting with the cocktail waitress, telling a joke or chatting with friends, watching the basketball game on a big screen TV located in a corner of the cardroom -- maybe even betting on the horse races while the game is underway.

PokerSharks generally sit down at the table with a reasonable starting stake -- at least 10 times the maximum allowable bet in a limit game. Thus, in a $2-$4 structured-limit seven-card stud game, your starting stake should be at least $40.00. I prefer to start with a buy-in of $50.00; while the casino may require a minimum buy-in of only five times the maximum bet, or $20.00 in this case As the game progresses, a PokerShark may experience some losses and his stack may shrink. But, when necessary, the PokerShark will add to the stack in order to ensure that he has sufficient funds (chips) to build a good size pot when the cards are "right" -- without having to go all in and thereby missing out on a golden opportunity to "earn" more $ with a strong winning hand.

Thus, a PokerShark generally will never be low on chips -- unless, perhaps, he is about to leave the game. On the other hand, PokerPigeons frequently will play with insufficient "capital" (chips) on the table in front of them; and, as a result, have to go all in quite often.

So, How Can You be Sure to Play at a "Good" Table?

Certainly, you don't want to get caught at a table filled with PokerSharks. In that case, it would be very difficult to come away a winner; furthermore, if you should win, the amount you win likely would not be very much. That's because PokerSharks go in at the start only with strong starting hands; i.e., they play relatively few hands. Only under certain conditions will they call with a marginal hand. (*See Chapter 3.*)

In addition, PokerSharks know how to "cut their losses" by folding when it is prudent to do so, and will drop out when holding an apparent losing hand rather than chasing. *(In fact, because of this, usually you can bluff out a PokerShark more easily than a PokerPigeon -- who is more prone to "keep you honest" by calling the bet when you attempt to pull off a bluff. But see also our discussion in Chapter 4 on a strategy dealing with betting on the last card -- on seventh street -- that can help you to avoid being bluffed out of a potentially winning hand.)*

If you can observe the active tables in the poker room before being seated, you can be more certain of starting off at a "good" table. Even if you do not have the opportunity to observe the tables before being seated, which is more often the case, you can use the same approach to make sure that you are playing at a table that is favorable for you -- where there is the right kind of "action."

How can you determine if it's a "good" table for you?

This is a very important question. Answering it correctly can make the difference between winning and losing. The answer to this question is so important that we will print it in bold face and put a box around it for added emphasis:

> **Observe the number of players making the opening bet and then staying in on fourth street:**
> • **If less than half of the players stay in on third street almost every hand, then this table may not be "right" for you.**
> • **If only two or three players usually stay in the hand on third street, then this table is not "right" for you.**
> • **If only two or three players usually stay in the hand on fourth street, then this table is not "right" for you.**

How to Do It. . .

Simply count the number of players going in on the opening bet on third street. With a full table of eight players, you want to see at least four players (including the forced bring-in bettor) putting their $ into the pot; occasionally three bettors is acceptable. Ideally, most of them should stay in on fourth street, too.

On the other hand, if only two or three out of a full table of seven or eight players consistently stay in on the opening bet -- and all the others drop out -- then there are too many PokerSharks at that table. You don't want to play there! Even if four or more players go in on third street but only two or three usually remain in on fourth street, there are too many PokerSharks -- not enough PokerPigeons. *(It's not likely, but perhaps there aren't any.)*

If you've been seated at such a "wrong" table and, if there are other tables at your stakes in the poker room, you need to change tables. Quietly and calmly get up from your seat, walk over to the floorperson or supervisor of the poker room, smile, and simply ask for a table change: "I'd like to change tables." He will acknowledge your request and make sure he knows where you are now seated.

You may have to wait for a seat to open up at another table. While you are waiting for the table change, be sure to play very conservatively. That means you must follow the other Basic Poker Rules very carefully and religiously. Permit yourself to make no deviations under any circumstances. You could also use this time to go to the rest room, or go for a walk to catch some fresh air, or have some lunch.

It is possible that, while you are waiting for the table change, the character of the table may change considerably. Players will leave and be replaced by others. Should this table then become a "good" table, then you no longer need the table change. If so, when you are informed

74

of an available seat at another table, you should simply respond, "I'll stay here. Thanks anyway." *(Always be polite.)*

It is also possible for a "good" table to turn "bad;" and, in that event, you may want to ask for a table change, as noted above. During the course of a poker session, it is not unlikely that the character of the table will change several times. Should you elect to remain at the table during those periods when the number of PokerSharks increases while the number of PokerPigeons decreases, you must exert even more care and patience as you follow the Basic Poker Rule #3 (see below).

Mike Caro, known as the "Mad Genius of Poker," has stated that poker tables are bound to change with time. "Tight" tables change because the better players leave or change to other tables, seeking more action and weaker opponents, and PokerPigeons leave the table after they go broke. Caro refers to this phenomenon as the "poker tide."

Adjusting Your Play

While you are observing the players and assessing the character of the table, you have a good opportunity to determine who are the PokerSharks and who are the Poker-Pigeons. That can be very important information! Make a mental note of this for use in future hands. You will then be able to make decisions and adjust your play accordingly, based on how each player is likely to be playing his hand. For example, when a PokerShark bets or raises, have respect for his hand and play cautiously. It is reasonable to assume that he is playing with poker rules and poker strategies similar to yours. Thus, on fifth street and beyond, you would be less prone to raise a bet made by a PokerShark than you would against a PokerPigeon.

If the PokerShark is still in the hand on fifth street and beyond, he is likely to be holding a strong hand, or drawing to one that likely would win the pot if he were to connect. And if he were holding a drawing hand, there would likely be several "outs" -- opportunities for improving his hand. Consider the following cases:

• With three-of-a-kind on fifth, sixth, or seventh streets, the PokerShark generally would bet -- unless he thinks someone has him beat. Simply call his bet if your cards warrant staying in the hand.

• If the PokerShark is drawing to a straight or flush, then he is more likely to check -- or just call if another player had bet. If the PokerShark has checked on fifth street, an aggressive bet would be proper -- provided your cards warrant a bet. Don't let him draw to a straight or flush too cheaply. And consider making a raise if another opponent had already bet.

Likewise, a PokerShark is undoubtedly more adept at pulling off a bluff. Accordingly, you would certainly want to call if he bet or raised on the river, assuming you were not beaten on the board; i.e., your hand has greater value -- or intrinsic worth -- than the one shown by the bettor based on his upcards.

It is usually good policy to call on the river if your hand is better than the opponents' upcards. At that point, there is usually a significant amount of money in the pot relative to the cost of the final bet; the pot odds are favorable. (See also Chapter 4.)

When playing against PokerPigeons, aggressive betting is usually recommended. *(To learn the strategy for aggressive playing, see Chapter 3.)* However, if you hold the "nuts" — a "sure-fire" winner — on fourth or fifth streets, and the PokerPigeons appear to have weak hands, checking or a small bet may keep them in the hand for another card, i.e., "slow-play." ("Sandbagging" or "check-raising." is checking with the intent to raise after someone else bets. Some poker players look down upon this type of play and would denigrate it. However, this is perfectly legal. It may permit you to extract the maximum $ from the PokerPigeon, which is your objective.) If his hand improves with the next card dealt, you may now be able to bet the maximum and get him to call all the way to the end.

**Avoid playing against PokerSharks.
It's best to play against PokerPigeons
— the more, the better.**

Opportunities:
A wise man will <u>make</u> more opportunities than he finds.
-- Francis Bacon

What About a Home Game?

A "home" poker game usually is a private game played at the home of one of the players. Often it is played around the kitchen or dining room table. *(Although, I once was involved in a monthly home game that was played in the back room of a local restaurant.)* The players usually know each other; some may be very close friends. You can play in a home game strictly as a social or business-related event; you can play to win $; or both.

Of course, if the game is strictly a social or business-related occasion, then it may not matter to you whether you win or lose.

I can recall one home game of poker while on a business trip many years ago with my then-boss, the general manager of a major division of a large aerospace company for which we worked. We were playing with a group of people from an important customer. My boss lost consistently. After the game, when we were alone, I commented to him that he had lost quite a "bundle." He acknowledged this with a knowing smile, and then told me that he wanted to lose -- and had played accordingly -- so that our customers would go home happy. They did indeed!

It goes without saying that, if you desire to win while playing in a home game, be sure that the other players are not more skilled than you. Otherwise, in the long run you are probably going to be their PokerPigeon. You certainly would not like that. If there happens to be several big PokerPigeons among the regular players, so much the better.

Accordingly, we might broaden the Basic Poker Rule #2 for winning at the game of poker:

> **Avoid competing against opponents who are better poker players than you.**

You may have some control over the selection of players in your home game. It will pay you to be discrete. If there are too many PokerSharks in your home game, it will be very difficult to be a consistent winner. In this sense, it is no different than playing in a public poker room, and selecting the table at which you play. Simply observe how many of the players go in hand after hand.

Remember, it is the players who determine the character of the poker table; to win you have to beat the other players. They may be good friends, but at the poker table, they become your opponents — friendly ones, of course. Generally speaking, you want to win whether playing in a casino or in a home game. Therefore the previous discussion should apply with regard to playing at a table that is "good" with respect to the number of PokerPigeons versus PokerSharks playing there.

Game selection is another important consideration in playing in a home game. Often the dealer chooses the game, and the deal rotates around the table from player to player. Whenever you can, you should select the game at which you have become expert and encourage others to do likewise. *(For me that game, of course, is seven-card stud.)* If they play many other poker games, you may not want to continue to participate in that home game -- unless you regard it solely as a social evening.

I used to play in a home game where the other players liked to play some of the wilder games -- other than seven-card stud. After a while, I decided to drop out of that game. It wasn't for me -- although I was a fairly consistent winner by applying the Basic Poker Rules and Poker Strategies to these other games.

* * *

Life is like a poker game.
It takes skill to succeed.
A little luck along the way also helps.
In both cases, the winner walks away
with the rewards.
-- George Epstein

80

What About Table Position?

While we are discussing the table selection, this is an opportunity to consider <u>table position</u>. What is the best seat at that table at which to play poker? Where should you prefer to be sitting with respect to the dealer and other players? There are considerations in this regard that can impact how you play a hand, how much you bet during the hand, and concomitantly how much you win -- or lose -- in any given hand.

Your seating position at the table is important.

In seven-card stud, the worst thing is to be seated at a position that makes it difficult for you to see all of the other players' upcards. (This is not a problem in Texas hold'em where all five upcards are placed in front of the dealer, near the center of the table.)

Lighting at the table is also a consideration; be sure that you can easily read your hole cards without having to lift them up from the table. You should be able to clearly see the cards when you raise the corner or edge nearest you, simultaneously shielding the cards from other players with your hands, while the rest of the card remains on the table.

Your comfort is important. When making key decisions, you don't want to be encumbered by an uncomfortable seat, a neighbor blowing cigarette smoke in your face, or an air conditioner blowing cold air at you. I also find it undesirable to be seated next to a player who frequently stands up while playing his hand. *(I have never seen a woman poker player do this -- only men.)* Fortunately it is rather rare. In such a case, I feel that I have to be extra cautious to be sure he doesn't see my hole cards while I am looking at them. That feeling in itself is an added restriction that I would prefer to avoid. The same is true when someone is seated behind one of the players, watching him during the game. (You might want to politely ask that person to move to the other side of that player, away from you.)

A key consideration is your position relative to the others seated at the table. There are advantages and disadvantages depending on the aggressiveness and skill of the other players.

Often you have no choice of seat; you are seated where there is an open place at the table a previous player had just left. *Sometimes it is wise to adjust your play depending on who is sitting to your right.*

But if you should have a choice of seat selection -- as when a game is about to start at the table, or if a preferred seat does become available when someone leaves the game -- then these are the factors to consider:

(1) If you have a vision problem so that it is difficult to see the upcards at one end of the table, especially if the table is large and oval-shaped, then it goes without saying that you want to be located at a middle seat where you can best see the upcards as they are dealt and during the betting. That

means, at a typical oval-shaped table, you prefer to sit opposite the dealer -- positions (seats No.) 3-6 in an eight-handed game. Seats No. 4 and 5 are best; while Seats No. 2 and 7 at the extreme ends of the oval-shaped table are the worst in this respect.

Your ability to see all of the upcards on the table should be the paramount consideration in selecting your seat. Otherwise, you are at a distinct disadvantage, and you are apt to make some mistakes.

Prediction: Someday, forward-looking poker rooms will use decks of cards that have large, oversized figures and numbers to accommodate older people and those with impaired vision. As more people live to ripe old ages, there will be greater demand for such decks. I once played in a home game with a man (a professor at a small college) who was legally blind; but using an oversized deck and with some help from the others at the table, he was able to play a fairly good game of poker. *(His fortitude and perseverance were admirable.)*

(2) If there is an especially aggressive player at the table -- one who raises often -- it is preferred to be seated to his left. From this position, generally you will be able to declare after that player. This will give you the opportunity to fold with marginal hands that might merit a call on a single bet, but not on a raised bet. The same is true for a very deceptive poker player; sit to his left if possible.

It is also desirable to be seated to the left of a PokerPigeon, so you can raise after he has bet, thereby increasing the size of the pot when you hold a strong hand.

If you are faced with a choice, it is preferred to be seated to the left of the very aggressive player. If the aggressive player happens to be a PokerPigeon also, so much the better.

(3) On the other hand, strictly from a playing standpoint, the seat immediately to the left of the dealer is preferred. In so-called "first position," or seat No. 1, you receive your cards before the other players. (This does not apply to Texas hold'em; see Chapter 5.) This allows you more time to assess your hand and observe the opponents' upcards as they are being dealt; and, if you are particularly astute, you may be able to observe your opponents' expressions and reactions as they receive their upcards. *(See Chapter 4 for strategy on "Using Tells.")*

Seat No. 1 or first position -- sometimes referred to as "first base" -- also affords you the opportunity to see what cards you "would have drawn" if you had stayed in, after having folded your hand. This serves to satisfy your curiosity. (But don't let curiosity engulf your attention so as to deter you from studying the play of your opponents. While you are sitting out a hand, always try to learn as much as you can about how your opponents play poker. That's more important than satisfying your curiosity as to what you might have made if you had stayed in the hand.)

The previous criteria should be the primary considerations in selecting your seat at the poker table. In seven-card stud, if viewing the cards is no problem for you, and you are not aware yet of the relative skills and aggressiveness or deceptiveness of the other players, then seat No. 1, just to the left of the dealer, is preferred.

After you have been at that table for a while and assessed the other players, don't hesitate to change your seat when a more desirable seat becomes available -- so you can be seated to the left of an aggressive player. You can do that quite simply by telling the dealer that you would like to change to that other seat, just as its present occupant is about to vacate it. If you believe a player is preparing to leave a preferred seat, immediately announce your intention to the dealer; otherwise another PokerShark is likely to beat you to the punch.

That happened to me once. A preferred seat to the left of a very aggressive PokerPigeon became available when its occupant left the game. I spoke up too late, and another player "captured" the preferred seat. He won a "bundle."

* * *

Intelligence:
All men see the same objects,
but all men do not equally understand them.
Intelligence is the tongue that discerns and tastes them.
-- Thomas Terhune; Centuries of Meditations

- **Rule #3**

DON'T LOSE!

PLAY ONLY THOSE HANDS
YOU HAVE A GOOD CHANCE OF WINNING

The third Basic Poker Rule for winning at the game of poker can be simply stated in two four-letter words. We'll state it this way so you will always remember it.

In the game of poker, this rule is the most important; although all of the rules must be followed to be a consistent winner. But, before you laugh because this rule as we initially state it seems so ridiculous and simple-minded, we will then restate the rule in more technical terms so that it can be better understood from a practical standpoint. And then we will explain the significance of this rule. In fact, Basic Poker Rule #3 is the most important rule in any gambling game if you want to come away a winner.

Basic Poker Rule #3 for winning at poker, simply stated, is:

DON'T LOSE!

Remember that!

Obviously, if you play poker and don't lose, then, it follows, you are going to win. *(Now, don't scoff at this. . .)*

As promised, we will now restate this important Basic Poker Rule #3 -- Don't Lose! -- so as to make it more meaningful and understandable:

> ## PLAY ONLY THOSE HANDS YOU HAVE
> ## A GOOD CHANCE OF WINNING

This rule is so important for winning at poker that I have capitalized all of the words for added emphasis! Now let's examine the meaning and significance of this rule so you can better implement it during the game.

Explanation:

To explain this Basic Poker Rule, let's assume that you are playing seven-card stud at a casino in Las Vegas with spread-limit stakes of $1 to $5. That is, the minimum bet is $1.00, and the maximum is $5.00 at any time. To start the game, you are dealt two downcards and one face up -- an upcard. At this point the betting starts with the player showing the lowest upcard forced to make at least a minimum bet -- the "bring-in." This is $1.00 in a $1-to-$5 game. The other players follow in turn, and make their declarations, i.e., call the bet, raise, or fold.

You are now about to make your most important decision for that hand. *(I cannot over-emphasize the importance of this decision.)* As you carefully examine your cards, ask yourself a very simple, but extremely important question -- the <u>key</u> question:

> ## *Do I have a good chance of winning with these cards?*

Answer this question properly and honestly if you want to be a winner. Don't allow yourself to be carried away with emotion. Just because the cards are "pretty" is no reason to "fall in love with them" and invest $ in a hand that should have been discarded at the outset. Once you make the initial investment, you are more likely to want to invest further as the game progresses.

To properly answer this very important question -- *Do I have a good chance of winning with these cards?* -- it is essential that you examine the upcards of your opponents in the game, while you study your own cards. How do their cards affect your hand? If you are holding a pair of sevens and you observe two other sevens in the opponents' upcards, do you want to stay in that hand? Of course not! Poker is a game of probabilities; so ask yourself:

> *"With these cards and considering the opponents' upcards -- cards which are no longer available to me -- do I have a reasonably good chance of making a hand that would likely win the pot?"*

After doing this, if the answer to our key question is "No, I do not have a good chance of winning," then you must turn your cards face down on the table and push them toward the center of the table, away from you and toward the dealer -- i.e., drop out; fold your cards, and wait for the next hand to be dealt. (Meanwhile, carefully observe the hand and how the opponents play their cards.)

This rule applies whether or not you are playing in a game of poker that has an ante. When there is no ante, as in Las Vegas-type low-limit ($1-$5) poker, it doesn't even cost you a single chip to wait for a more favorable playing hand. When there is an ante, there may be some marginal holdings that warrant a call under certain conditions; we will explore this situation later.

With just three cards dealt to you -- the two down-cards and one face up, there are only certain combinations that can occur:

- Three-to-a-Straight
- Three-to-a-Flush
- Three-of-a-Kind
- A Pair
- No combination/No matching cards

With three-of-a-kind -- three cards of the same value -- certainly you will always want to stay in the hand, no matter their rank.

In poker parlance, when you are dealt three-of-a-kind at the start, two cards in the hole and one up, all of the same value, they are said to be "rolled up." Three-of-a-kind also is sometimes referred to as "trips" or "triplets." Three aces is great!

On the opposite extreme, with three cards that do not match, showing no combination of interest, you certainly want to fold without any further ado. Examples of such "no-combination/no-matching-cards" hands are Q♣ 10♦ 5♥, or K♠ 9♣ 8♥, or even A♥ 10♣ 5♣. You can be assured that you will be dealt far more of these than of the more desirable combinations that might merit a stay-in decision. So you can expect to fold many more hands than you play -- perhaps as many as 7 to 10 on the average, for each hand worthy of calling the opening bet.

As noted above, with three-of-a-kind for your first three cards, you will always stay in. But, with the other combinations listed above, there will be many situations when you should drop out of the hand. Let's examine each of these other combinations to illustrate this rule -- whether to stay in or to fold.

Remember, at this point we are discussing only whether it is prudent to stay in the hand, not how best to play the hand. Depending on the specifics of the hand, there will be various strategies on how best to play the hand to optimize your chances of taking the pot and winning as much money as possible; these will be discussed in Chapters 3 and 4.

Certainly, if your three cards bear no relationship to one another -- regardless of your opponents' upcards --

90

it is quite obvious this is not likely to lead to a winning hand. You would not want to stay in and invest any of your money in such a hand (even if there were an ante) -- although some PokerPigeons might do so. For example, a J-6-2 in three different suits would never qualify as an opening hand. Nor, as a general rule, would a A-J-7 -- even if two of the cards were suited, i.e., both in the same suit. *(This latter is a marginal hand, and there are times when such a hand should be played. Playing too many marginal hands can be costly; in general, you will lose more $ by investing in such hands than you win on those occasions when one develops into the best hand at the table. PokerPigeons play much too many marginal hands! We will discuss marginal hands below, and a strategy related to the playing of marginal hands in Chapter 3.)*

To reiterate, it is extremely important to understand when -- and why -- you should stay in and call the opening bet on third street. When do your cards warrant the investment? We will define and discuss the combinations that permit you to stay in. Remember each player has been dealt two cards down -- in the "hole" -- and one upcard. Now you must make that all-important decision whether to stay in the hand or fold. At this point, let's consider each of the combinations listed above, with the exception of the two extreme cases, three-of-a-kind and no-combination, which we have already covered. (We will also give examples of marginal opening hands which, as will be discussed later, may be played under certain conditions.)

Carefully look at all of your opponents' upcards; note whether any of the cards you need to make the straight are already dealt out to the other players -- and, hence, no longer available for your use. Remember, it takes five cards to make a straight. . .

By way of illustration, suppose you hold J-10-9 unsuited. You have three cards in sequence to a straight, and it is open at both ends; i.e., you can catch cards at both ends of the sequence to help fill the straight. In this case, you should stay in the hand so long as there are not a lot of 7s, 8s, Qs, and Ks already showing in your opponents' upcards. There should be no more than one each 8 or queen exposed. (One of these cards is needed to make it four to a straight in sequence.) Otherwise your chances of making the straight are vastly diminished. Preferably you would also like to see no more than one -- two at most -- of the 7s and kings exposed for the same reason.

Suppose you hold A-2-3 unsuited. They are in sequence. Should you stay in? No way! You do not have an opening hand because it is not open at both ends; fold your cards and observe the game while you wait for the next hand to be dealt. Be patient! Remember that patience is a very essential ingredient to being a winning poker player.

Patience is like the flour that is used to bake bread: You will not be successful without it.

Exceptions

There are always exceptions to any rule. For example, if you were dealt A-K-Q of different suits, you have a three-card sequence that is not open at both ends -- just as was the case with the A-2-3. However, in this case the cards are all very high in value. If there are very few of your matching cards -- aces, kings and queens -- showing in the opponents' upcards, it may be worth an opening call based on the chance of making a high two pair or better. This is especially true if you are one of the last to declare on the opening round of betting, or if there are no high upcards yet to declare after your turn -- so a raise is not likely. But fold if there is any heavy betting or raising. With heavy betting or raising, the assumption is that the heavy bettor/raiser already has a high pair, perhaps even three-of-a-kind, and you would still have to look for your high pair.

There is another possible exception to this rule. Let's say that you do hold three-to-a-straight in sequence, open at both ends, and "your" cards are live; but in this case the opening player, seated to your left, bets $3.00 rather than $1.00, and the next player raises it to $6.00. Everyone folds and it is now your turn to declare. Drawing to a straight can be quite expensive. In order for this hand to be a viable investment, there needs to be several players in the hand to build up the pot -- in case you make the straight (and win). If there are only one or two other players remaining in the pot, you should consider folding your cards unless your three-to-a-straight in sequence includes high cards that could develop into a strong hand even if you did not make the straight.

Should I Raise?

While we are only discussing the decision whether to stay in or fold in this case, it is appropriate that we consider the option of raising on third street when you hold three-to-a-straight in sequence. Don't raise! You do not want to force opponents out at this point; you want to build as large a pot as possible in case you make the straight -- a likely winning hand. With three-to-a-straight or three-to-a-flush (see below), the more opponents remaining in the hand, the more $ you can expect to win -- when/if you make the straight or flush.

The three indispensables of genius are understanding, feeling, and perseverance. The three things that enrich genius are contentment of mind, the cherishing of good thoughts, and exercising the memory. -- Southey

You might think that this rule should not require much explanation -- but it does. Any three cards of the same suit offer the potential for making a flush. More likely than not, a flush is usually -- but not always, of course -- a winner. Therefore, this holding would appear worthy of a call on third street. And if your three-to-a-flush includes one or more high cards -- ace, king, or queen, all the better.

But there are times you should fold your cards after being dealt three-to-a-flush. That may seem contrary to good judgment, but sometimes folding such a hand is prudent and will save you $. Let's illustrate this with an example of a three-card holding that frequently occurs. You are playing in a $1-to-$5 seven-card stud game, and you have been dealt, say, three spades. Should you stay in? The answer: *That depends. . .*

Look at the your opponents' upcards. What do you see? If you observe four other spades exposed in the opponents' upcards, what conclusion should you draw? (The same is true if you see three other spades exposed unless, perhaps, you have an ace, a king. or a queen.)

Let's examine this situation: You are on third street with four more betting rounds yet to come. Your chances of making the flush are not good. Why is that? Consider that seven of the thirteen spades are already in play -- your three spades and the four in the opponents' upcards; that leaves only six more spades available. You need to catch two of the remaining six spades. The chance of that happening is not high enough to warrant a large $ investment that would likely be required if you were to stay in the hand all the way to the river.

For the sake of discussion, suppose you had a foolish hunch and decided to stay in with your three-spades-to-a-flush, and caught a fourth spade on sixth street. We'll also assume that only one other spade fell in one of the opponent's upcards up to that point. Now there are just four spades left in the deck -- assuming none are in the other players' downcards, in the "muck," or in the burn cards. So, at best you have four chances out of the remaining cards, of which there are approximately 30, to be dealt another spade on the river. Those are not attractive odds -- 6.5-to-1 against you.

Explanation

To understand our calculation, first consider the cards you can see: your two downcards plus all of the upcards dealt to the eight players at the table; that's ten cards. We will make a few reasonable assumptions for this calculation. Assuming that on fourth, fifth and sixth streets, four players had stayed in the hand, so that 12

96

additional upcards — three to each player — were dealt on the board. Altogether there are now 22 cards which you can see. Of the remaining 30 cards (52 - 22), there are 26 that are not spades versus only four cards that are spades. Therefore the odds against making the flush are:

$$26/4 = 6.5/1$$

Meanwhile you will have made a considerable investment in that hand. You will have called bets and possibly one or more raises on fourth, fifth and sixth streets. And, at that point, the size of the pot may have grown sufficiently to warrant a call on seventh street because the pot odds* may be higher than 6.5 to 1. There would now have to be at least $33.00 (6.5 x $5.00 = $32.50) in the pot to warrant a call of a $5.00 bet in the hope of catching the flush on seventh street. And that assumes no one raises, in which case it would cost you further. The chances are that you would not make the flush — thereby significantly reducing your stack of chips unless you "luck out." The odds are very much against you.

This explains why generally it would be prudent to fold that hand back on third street. With three or more of your matching cards showing in the opponents' upcards, fold that three-to-a-flush hand before it has cost you any significant amount of money.

---

* The pot odds are the ratio of the amount of money in the pot relative to the amount of the bet required to call and stay in the hand. The "implied" odds are the ratio of the amount you could win, including money bet in subsequent rounds, relative to your cost to call the present bet.

Make good use of your time while waiting by observing your opponents and the playing of the hand. See if you can analyze their hands based on their play and response to the cards dealt. What do you think each player is holding? If there is a showdown at the end, try to observe the cards with which each remaining player called the opening bet -- so you can better understand how he plays. Look for "tells" -- characteristics displayed by your opponents that may give you clues as to the nature of the hands they may be holding or how they play.

An Exception

Having convinced you of the wisdom of folding that hand, now let me offer an exception to this rule. In this same situation, if you can get in "cheap" on third street with a minimum bet, it would be well worth a small investment to see if you might catch the fourth spade on fourth street. (You are investing/betting on the potential value of your cards.) There is approximately one chance out of four that you will be dealt a fourth spade. If that were to happen, then you would have a hand with a strong potential -- needing only one more spade for the flush, with three cards yet to draw. If you are the last to bet on third street -- or you are reasonably certain no one declaring after you will raise -- and the bet is the $1.00 minimum bring-in (with no raises), in that case a call bet of $1.00 would be a reasonable investment.

Let's consider another related situation: You are dealt three small-to-medium clubs -- no high cards -- and only two other clubs are exposed in the opponents' up-cards. Should you stay in? What is your decision?

<u>Answer</u>: You should stay in only if you can get in with a minimum bet. *(This is an example of a marginal opening hand.)*

On the other hand, in this same case, if your cards include one or more high cards -- an ace, king or queen -- and none of these is exposed in your opponents' upcards, stay in even if the bet is raised. The difference here is that, even if the flush does not develop, you have a high card that could pair up or better. You have "outs" -- opportunities to improve the hand -- in addition to the flush draw.

Let's take this case one step further. Say you are dealt A-8-6 of clubs with only two other clubs showing in the opponents' upcards. Generally this hand certainly would be worth calling the opening bet. However, if there are two or more of "your"* matching high card exposed in the opponents' upcards (i.e., in this example, if you saw two more aces out), that should encourage you to fold if there is any heavy betting or raising. The reason for this distinction is that the high cards provide an opportunity to make a high hand even if the flush were not to develop. But if two of these already are "dead" for you, your chances of pairing up are not good. Stay in, of course, with a minimum bet -- but consider folding if the betting is raised. *(This is another example of a marginal opening hand.)*

---

* In using the terms "your," "your suit," and "your cards," we refer to the cards or suit you need to improve your hand.

If your three suited cards are low in value -- nothing higher than an eight -- you should call the opening bet only if no more than two of "your suit" are showing among your opponents' upcards, and the bet is the minimum bring-in. *(This is another example of a marginal opening hand.)* However, if your three suited cards also are in sequence and "open" at both ends -- e.g., 5-6-7 of hearts -- you should stay in even with three of "your suit" exposed because of the added opportunity to make a straight -- unless there are a lot of fours and eights (cards you need to make the straight) exposed in the opponents' upcards. Again, if there is heavy betting or raising, drop out.

> • **Stay in if you have a pair of aces or kings.**
> • **Stay in if you have a medium-to-high pair -- eights or higher -- and none of "your cards" are showing in the opponents' upcards.**

If you hold a pair of aces or kings, stay in even if your matching cards -- other aces or kings -- are showing in the opponents' upcards. *(We will discuss the proper strategy for playing such a hand in Chapter 3.)*

But if you have been dealt a pair of queens or lower, and a matching card is showing among the opponents' up-cards, you now have a marginal opening hand and should consider folding. Needless to say, if you hold a pair of queens (or lower), and your "neighbor" shows a third queen as his upcard, then your chance of making three queens -- a likely winning hand -- is very poor. If both of the other queens are still available ("live"), you have twice the chance of "hitting" than if only one queen is still in the deck. One might argue that even with both other queens exposed, you could make two pair, queens-up -- and that could be a winner. Yes, that certainly is true; but the player with the aces or kings would beat you if he makes two pair also -- and, of course, many other hands beat two pair. You would likely have to make a considerable $ investment during the play of that hand; and the probability of ending up with the highest hand is not high enough to warrant such a large investment.

Many poker experts would argue that such a hand should be played in a tight game -- where there is not any heavy betting and raising. However, consider this: To make that hand worth playing you would need to make a large raise on third street so as to reduce the number of opponents. Especially in a tight game, only an opponent with a strong hand -- one that could easily beat you -- would likely stay in by calling your raise. And if everyone folds, you will not have earned many chips by your raise. You have more to lose than to gain in this case.

On the other hand, in this same situation, if there are a few loose players or PokerPigeons (especially "calling stations" -- PokerPigeons who call all bets no matter what) at your table, you might consider staying in and raising on third street. Force out the tight players with marginal or drawing hands, and hope that one of the remaining players doesn't draw out on you.

Remember at this point we are addressing the opening bet and whether or not you should stay in the hand. See Chapters 3 and 4 for the betting/calling/raising strategies.

We will examine the playing of two-pair hands later; suffice it to say that, other than aces-up or kings-up, two pair is not a very strong hand and could cost you more $ than it "earns." So it is prudent to try to avoid such situations from the beginning by following this rule.

To further emphasize this important rule by illustration, consider the following typical hand:

I held a jack in the hole along with a deuce, with a second jack as my first upcard. That is, I was dealt a split pair of jacks with a deuce "kicker." However -- and this is the key factor -- a third jack showed among the opponents' upcards. Anticipating a raised bet by one of the opponents to my left, I dropped out -- as I should have, according to this rule. *(I would have stayed in only for a minimum opening bet.)*

I then observed the subsequent cards as they were dealt to determine what hand I might have received if I had not thrown in my cards. The next card that would have been dealt to me was another deuce; I would have made two pair, jacks over deuces. A player seated to my right, showing a queen up, was high on the board, and came out betting the maximum. Two other players called his bet.

Under these circumstances, what are the chances that I would have held the winning hand? We won't try to calculate the mathematical odds. Let's assume I stayed in with the two pair, jacks and deuces, calling all bets and possibly a few raises, hoping to make a full house.

Most likely, I would have held a losing hand at the close of the deal -- perhaps the second-best hand, losing to two pair, queens-up, or possibly to an even better hand held by one of the other players who called in the face of the strong betting and raising. That would have been a costly hand for me had I decided to stay in and call the opening bet holding a pair of jacks with a third jack already out. (Yes, there is always the chance that I would have caught the case jack or even filled up for a full house; but, remember, the probabilities would be very much against me in that case.)

As noted above, starting with a pair of aces or kings is a good opening hand. You should call the opening bet even if one of "your cards" is showing in the opponents' upcards. The reason for this is that, even though you are less likely to make three aces, there is a good chance you will make two pair -- aces-up or kings-up. If you play these hands properly, you will often take the pot. *(See Chapters 3 and 4 for pertinent strategies for playing such hands.)*

An ace is a playing card marked with a single pip on its center. But to golf players, it's a score of one stroke on a hole; and to tennis players, an ace is a point won on the serve. And, during a war, an ace is a pilot who shoots down five or more enemy airplanes. What's more, if we say that someone is an "ace," that's a way of saying that s/he excels. Now that makes good sense: Give me lots of aces, and I'll excel too!

-- from "The Unusual Language of Poker" by George Epstein; *Poker Digest*, August 10, 2000.

> • **Stay in if you hold a small pair, sevens or lower, only if :**
> **(1) none of the cards matching your pair is showing in the opponents' upcards;**
> **(2) you have a high "kicker" card; and**
> **(3) not more than one of your "kicker" shows up in the opponents' upcards.**

All three conditions must be satisfied if you are to stay in the hand with a small pair — sevens or under. First of all, none of your matching cards for the pair should be showing in the opponents' upcards. Second, your third card — the "kicker" — must be a jack or higher. Third, if more than one of your "kicker" card shows up as an opponent's upcard, you should fold this hand unless you can call the opener with a minimum bet. With a minimum bet, it makes good sense to make a small investment in order to see if you can improve your hand on fourth street; if it does not improve, then you should fold unless everyone checks or, perhaps, if there is only a minimum bet to call.

This is very important; I've lost many a hand in order to learn and understand it. By way of illustration, consider the most extreme case: a pair of deuces in the hole with a trey up. What are the chances of this starting hand emerging as a winner? Not very good, and certainly not worth the investment you would have to make to find out. And, if it should turn out to be the winner, the pot is not likely to be very large.

Let's discuss this hand to explain our rationale. To begin with, a holding of a pair of deuces and a trey is not much higher in value than an A-3. But in the case of the A-3 (two cards), you still have five more cards to draw to help improve the hand -- versus only four more cards with the pair of deuces-trey (three cards) hand; and, furthermore, a second ace would give you a pair of aces, a strong playing hand.

Starting with a pair of deuces, the best hand you could reasonably hope for (aside from eventually filling up) would be three deuces. What are the chances of getting the third deuce? (Of course, four deuces is possible, but highly unlikely.)

There are two deuces left in the deck. Assuming there are 40 cards still available, your chance of being dealt a third deuce on the next card would be 2/40 -- 5 percent. The odds improve somewhat for each succeeding card dealt -- providing a deuce does not show up in an opponent's upcards -- but remain relatively low.

And, even if you are fortunate enough to catch the third deuce, you may still be beat by a higher three-of-a-kind (there are twelve other "trips" possible) or a straight or flush in an opponent's hand..

More likely, you may make two pair. But with a low "kicker" card (the trey, in this example), the most likely two pair would be treys and deuces. That's a very weak hand! You would probably throw such a hand away if there were any substantial betting, and play only if it was very cheap to do so -- provided most of your needed cards were still available and not showing in your opponents' upcards.

Let's assume you felt "lucky" *(we're only human, after all)* and made the mistake of staying in "on a hunch" and actually made three deuces -- and it is the best hand. Most likely there would be very little money in the pot.

Here's why: If there had been a strong hand in the game, there probably would have been some heavy betting and/or raising. Of course, in that case, you would wisely have dropped out of the hand. If you happened to make the three deuces early in the hand (perhaps on fourth street), you would have -- quite properly -- bet the maximum or raised to chase out the possible straight and flush draws and higher pairs in order to improve your chances of winning with your small three-of-a-kind. The net result is there would be a rather small pot for you to win -- if you were lucky.

Let's briefly consider another example to further explain this rule. Suppose, on third street, you are dealt a pair of fives with an ace "kicker." There are no fives showing in the opponents' upcards; that's good. But there are two aces showing in the other players' upcards; that's not good.

Basic Poker Rule #3 requires that you fold this hand. Your chance of making aces-up is not good; at most, there is only the case ace left in the deck. Of the 42* remaining, unseen cards, only one of them is an ace. You don't have to calculate the mathematical odds to realize that staying in with such a hand would be a very poor investment -- unless there was only a minimum bet to call.

These examples are intended to help emphasize the importance of this rule:

> **Stay in if you hold a small pair only if none of your matching cards is showing in your opponents' upcards and you have a high "kicker" card, with no more than one showing in your opponents' upcards.**

As noted above, we have been discussing only whether to stay in the hand or fold after the first three cards are dealt. We have not addressed the important question of how to best play the hand. Suppose the decision -- based on the rule -- is to stay in the pot. How should you play the hand? Should you simply call? Should you raise? Should you try to bluff? The answers to these questions are part of our discussion on the Poker Strategies for Winners to be explored at length in Chapters 3 and 4.

---

* On the deal, you see your two downcards and all of the upcards; that's a total of 10 cards at a table with eight players. That leaves 42 cards that are unseen (52 - 10).

Basic Poker Rule #3 is essential to being a winning poker player. If you do not abide by this rule, you will not be a winner -- certainly not in the long run. In fact, you may be a PokerPigeon for the other players at your table. Therefore, I offer the following suggestion:

Suggestion:

• **When you get ready to sit down to play poker, even before you even purchase a stack of chips, think of Basic Poker Rule #3:**

Don't Lose!

That's easy to remember.
Think about it during the game too.

• **And then recall the technical terminology to describe this rule:**

Play only those hands you have a good chance of winning.

This Basic Poker Rule is by far the most important rule for winning poker players. Read over and over the above discussions on the various combinations of opening hands; think about them; know and understand them so well that they almost become an integral part of your psyche and of your natural thought process.

Gambling and Investing

In concluding our discussion on the Basic Poker Rules #1 - #3, it is useful to recognize and admit that poker is a form of gambling. It is a risky undertaking. You are betting; you are wagering; and you certainly are speculating. You are risking your $ in order to try to win some $ from your opponents. It can be hazardous.

But there is another dimension. To a large extent, playing the game of poker is a form of investing. You are committing $ in order to gain a financial return. In addition, you are committing your time and energy toward this same goal. By using the Basic Poker Rules, you are better prepared to make your investment. Every investment has an element of risk. Generally, the greater the risk, the higher the potential return. But an informed investor can minimize the risk, and a shrewd investor can take steps to maximize the returns.

The Basic Poker Rules will help you to minimize the risk. And, after you have learned the Poker Strategies, you will then be in a better position to maximize the return on your investment.

Never do card tricks
for the people with whom you play poker.

- **Rule #4:**

BE ALERT!
**DON'T DRINK ALCOHOLIC BEVERAGES
OR USE DRUGS WHILE PLAYING POKER;
DON'T PLAY POKER IF YOU ARE TIRED
OR DISTURBED**

Surely you would not drink and drive a vehicle. Alcohol dulls one's senses and ability to think clearly. Drinking alcoholic beverages while playing poker is likely to cause you to make some poor decisions or outright blunders. After all, it is well known that alcohol reduces your inhibitions; it makes you less cautious — more willing to take unwise risks. That can be quite costly in a game of poker.

Many casinos make alcoholic beverages readily available for the players. *(But note that the dealer isn't offered any.)* In some casinos, as in Las Vegas, the drinks are complimentary. *(The casinos more than make up for the cost of the drinks. It is to the advantage of the casino, because you will then probably stay longer at the table — and that means more revenue for the casino.)* Every twenty minutes or so, the cocktail waitress comes to your table and asks if anyone would like a drink. You are thirsty, and a drink would be refreshing — besides it's "on the house." What a deal!

<u>Resist the temptation</u>. Drink a coke or coffee, or refresh yourself with a glass of fruit juice if you're thirsty. *(I like a mix of cranberry juice and orange juice. Besides,*

it's healthy.) Go get a drink of water. Stretching your legs and getting a breath of fresh air can be invigorating. In any case, taking an occasional break is good practice.

The only time it is considered permissible for a good poker player to accept an alcoholic beverage is when he is ready to leave for his room to rest (or sleep) or about to go to dinner. You might even take the drink with you when you leave the game.

Drugs, even many prescribed by your medical doctor, can affect your alertness. Don't play poker while taking such drugs. If the container warns against driving a vehicle or operating equipment while taking this medication, then you shouldn't be playing poker either. By all means, take your medication if the doctor has prescribed it for you, but do it after you play -- not while you are playing poker.

Likewise, if you find yourself rather tired, the time is long past that you should have excused yourself from the game and gone to your room to rest or sleep. Playing when you are tired is bound to cause you to make a mistake now and then. Certainly it will make you less alert and less likely to win! The same precautions apply to being hungry or emotionally disturbed for any reason. Don't play poker in such cases. It is a big mistake to play poker if you are angry for some reason. If you are hungry, satisfy this need before you try to concentrate on playing poker.

Drinking and playing poker don't mix!

111

Comments

<u>Expect to Lose Sometimes; Try to Avoid/Minimize Losses</u>

We have now covered the four Basic Poker Rules for winning at the game of poker. These rules apply to all poker games wherever played -- with or without an ante. If you abide by these rules, you are bound to be a winner in the long run. But, remember, inherent in playing by these rules is having patience. To play by the rules, you must have patience; be willing to sit out many more hands than you play. That is important. Our Basic Poker Rules are intended to help you win most of the time (not every time because of the element of luck). In Chapters 3 and 4, we will discuss the Poker Strategies. These are designed to further enhance your chances of winning and to optimize the amount of your $ winnings when you do win.

Surely, there can be no guarantee that you will win every time you play. In fact, it is certain that you will lose on occasion if you play poker often enough. You are doing very well if you win two out of three sessions; that means you will have won twice as many times as you lose. Better yet, if you can win 75 percent of the sessions! There is an element of luck. There will be times when you get good hands and play them just right -- but lose to better hands. Coming in second-best in poker can be very expensive. Manage and control your money so that you never lose more than you think you can afford, and so that you have more than enough money to stake your next session at the poker table. Never go into debt to play poker.

The rules and strategies will help you avoid and minimize the losses, but losing happens to the best of poker players. When things seem to be going wrong for you, if you are "off" your game, if you believe you are playing "out of your element" and feel uncomfortable -- that's the time to pick up your remaining chips and leave the table; cash in your chips and wait for another session. That's easier said than done. It takes good self-discipline to recognize when you shouldn't be playing poker at that table at that time, and have the courage to quit before you lose more.

Likewise, if you have been winning and the cards "turn cold" for you, it may be time to leave the game. Are you having a run of "bad luck," or is it that you are getting tired and not playing as well as you should or could. In either case, it would be prudent to quit while you are still ahead. It's always wise to leave the table a winner. . .

(At this point, I would suggest you review the discussion about Money Management, as part of the Basic Poker Rule #1.)

If you are working for a living, you are pleased to get a raise in pay. But if you're playing poker, you may not appreciate it when another player puts in a "raise" at the table.
-- from "The Unusual Language of Poker" by George Epstein;
Poker Digest, August 10, 2000.

Falling in Love

Implicit in following the Basic Poker Rule #3 is the following admonition:

Don't fall in love with your cards.

You look at the cards dealt to you. "Gosh," you say, "they are beautiful -- lots of pretty pictures and high cards too!" Your hand is so beautiful -- so beautiful, in fact, that you may feel inclined almost to embrace the cards, hold them tightly, caress them tenderly, keep them, and play them to the very end.

Beware. . . Playing poker is an investment -- just like buying a stock. Playing poker is not a romance! Not a wedding. Not even a romantic interlude. Unless the cards are really meaningful and offer a reasonable probability of leading to a winning hand, you want to discard them like any other undesirable combination of cards dealt to you. The sooner you get rid of them, the better.

"Falling in love" with the cards is a rather common failing of many PokerPigeons -- and you always want to be a PokerShark, never a PokerPigeon!

If we had no winter, the spring would not be so pleasant;
if we did not sometimes taste of adversity,
prosperity would not be so welcome.   -- Anne Bradstreet

Letting Others Influence Your Style of Play

How your opponents play their hands is bound to influence your own playing. You are likely to tend to play somewhat looser if you are at a table with a lot of very loose players who bet and raise almost with abandon, and rarely fold their cards. They crave action! Loose players will win more hands than you -- because they play many more hands; but, concomitantly, they will lose more hands too. In the final analysis, they will be losers.

Let us be thankful for the fools.
But for them the rest of us could not succeed. -- Mark Twain

Actually, you should continue to play according to the Basic Poker Rules and Poker Strategies, and be less inclined to try to bluff out a loose player. He is not likely to fold. If a loose player wants to bet or raise and build a pot for you, by all means, grant him that opportunity.

It is prudent to call a loose player at the showdown on seventh street, unless you are beat by his board cards. Loose players will bet with a weak hand, and try to bluff quite often. If your hand is higher than your opponent's upcards, it is usually wise to call on the final bet. *(See strategies for betting on the river in Chapter 4.)*

A table full of very loose players is ideal; you are more apt to win a big pot when you make a powerful hand, and that is what Basic Poker Rule #3 helps you to do.

Likewise, if the table has many very tight players, your natural instinct may lead you to play according to their pattern. Don't. Stick to the four Basic Poker Rules and the Poker Strategies. Tight players bet only if they hold a strong hand. A table full of very tight players is not a good table. According to Basic Poker Rule #2, you should change tables or play very conservatively while waiting for a change.

If there are only one or two tight players at your table, remain seated. How should you adjust your playing when you find yourself ensconced in a hand with one of them as your sole opponent? Certainly you want to play according to the Basic Poker Rules and Strategies. However, it is proper to play somewhat more aggressively -- but not loose* -- against a tight player if you want to force him to fold when his hand does not improve. At the same time, respect his bets and raises. Tight players rarely bluff. Tight players sometimes check and raise. Call only if your hand could take the pot or if you have a number of good "outs" (live cards that would substantially improve your hand), and the pot odds are favorable. If a tight player raises, the odds of making your hand must be much higher than the pot odds to justify a call.

---

* Loose playing is the opposite of tight (very conservative) playing. A loose player will stay in with marginal hands and even poorer ones, no matter the circumstances. And he is likely to call all raises as long as there is a chance to catch a needed card. On the other hand, an aggressive player will bet and raise, even reraise when his cards are favorable.

A rather common failing is to alter your style of play when you observe an opponent betting/raising, and he is winning hand after hand. He is being overly aggressive, perhaps playing loosely, and is winning. If he is so successful in this tactic, then, you reason, you ought to follow his example so you can win lots of $ too. Isn't that right? Wrong! Play by the four Basic Poker Rules and Poker Strategies; stick to them and be not tempted to stray. *(Believe me; I have tried it, and it just doesn't work -- at least not in the long run.)*

More likely than not, before the game is done, that overly-aggressive player whose stack of chips has been growing rapidly will become a loser. Sometimes you can watch his stack of chips rise and then fall *(like the Roman Empire!),* sometimes precipitously -- a giant tidal wave! *(One of the Poker Strategies will teach you the proper way to play aggressively.)*

Controlled and selective-aggressive playing is recommended -- but certainly not overly-aggressive playing. The overly-aggressive player bluffs often -- much too often. He might actually be very loose, betting and raising with inferior hands. Proper aggressive playing allows an occasional but discrete bluff; it also encourages betting or raising the maximum when it is appropriate to do so, as when you believe that you hold the best hand or, at least, a very strong hand that is likely to make you the winner. You may raise to chase other players out of the pot -- when it is appropriate to do so. And you may raise to maximize your winnings. Proper aggressive playing also allows you to bet

117

when you are high on board provided certain conditions are satisfied. *We will discuss this aspect when we review the Poker Strategies for Winners.*

Generally, overly-aggressive players are loose players who tend to bluff much too often. Frequent bluffing is an integral part of their style of play. If you have identified an opponent as an overly-aggressive player, be prepared to call his bets if your cards are not beaten on the board. In fact, if you feel certain your hand is better, a raise may be in order. He may even call and afford you an extra bet to add to your profit.

But do not be surprised if there is another raise. On one occasion, I had a full house, aces-full of kings -- an extremely powerful hand. Indeed, you might call it a "monster" hand! An overly-aggressive loose player raised me on seventh street, showing three cards to both a flush and a straight on the board. I figured him for a flush; there were no pairs in his upcards, so he wasn't likely to have four-of-a-kind. So I reraised. He smiled as he reraised again. I paused to think: It was possible that he held a straight flush -- not likely, but certainly possible. So I just called. Sure enough, he had caught the straight flush on the river. I was devastated! That's what is called a "bad beat" -- a very strong hand losing to a very unlikely draw.

Luck comes and goes. . .
Knowledge stays forever.
-- Bill Burton; About.com Casino Gambling Guide

118

How to Dress for the Poker Game

One thing that is rarely discussed is how you should dress while playing poker. The casino may have a dress code requiring a player's clothing be such as not to offend other players. I suggest that you dress comfortably but in good taste.

On occasion, I have seen men wearing neckties while playing poker; this is not recommended. A player is more comfortable unencumbered by a tie around his neck, and hence better able to concentrate on the game itself.

A casual, comfortable style of clothing is recommended, preferably neat, and not wrinkled nor food-stained. Since most poker rooms are air conditioned, a light jacket or sweater may be useful; just hang it over the back of your chair if you don't need it.

I have also seen more than one woman dressed in revealing clothing -- her bust almost fully exposed as she leaned over the table; that may be fine for her, but it may be distracting to some of the males at the table. *(Perhaps that was her idea.)* If nothing else, as a courtesy to other players, such clothing should not be worn at the poker table.

The casino may also impose some regulations on the clothing worn within its premises. These would not conflict with our recommendations.

Food at the Poker Table

Some poker rooms allow you to eat at the table; some forbid it. I have observed players eating a full meal while continuing to play their hands. I do not recommend this practice. Concentrate on the game; it's a big enough job without being distracted by the process of eating. It's okay to sip on a cup of coffee or a coke while playing, or even to enjoy a candy sucker -- but not a meal. Turn your seat away from the table and announce to the dealer that you will be out of the game for a short time while eating your meal. Relax and enjoy it. (Of course, if you were paying for time at the table, it would be prudent to wait till your time was up and then leave for your meal.)

One might question the wisdom of eating food while playing at the table. Those casinos that allow it, require that the food be located on a cart just behind the player, so he must turn away from the table while eating. That certainly would impair his ability to concentrate fully on the game. There is also a matter of good health practices. It is not advisable to handle the cards and chips, and the food too. There could be germs or bacteria on the cards or chips. And the playing cards may be sullied by food-soiled hands.

* * *

Advice for every day: *Be orderly and systematic; Be helpful; Be happy in what you do; Listen to others; Enjoy your work; Learn to relax; Be constructive; Help another person; Harm no person; Be considerate of others; Every day is a beautiful day...* **And have a good day today.** -- Anonymous

CHAPTER THREE – POKER STRATEGIES FOR WINNERS: HOW TO WIN MORE OFTEN AND WIN MORE $

What do we mean when we speak of a strategy for winning at poker?

When military commanders prepare a strategy, they are defining a plan or course of action to take against an enemy. The objective is to enhance their chance of besting the enemy by winning the battle or the war.

They carefully assess all of the prevailing and pre-sumed conditions, including information gathered from hopefully reliable intelligence sources, and try to select those conditions that will be most favorable for their forces versus those of the enemy. In other words, they want to optimize the probability of a victory. And then, consider-ing all this information, they plan their actions, step by step, while anticipating the possible reactions of the enemy in response to each action.

It's no different than playing a game of checkers or chess. Before you make your move, you should consider the possible responses of your opponent -- and make sure your move will lead to the end you desire.

When a football team plans a strategy, it tries to take advantage of its strengths and to minimize its weaknesses. The coaches study the opposing team and make plans so as to take advantage of its weaknesses and overcome its strengths. Very likely, the team has been scouting the opponent by having its representatives watch the opposing team perform in previous games. For example, if you, as the coach, know that the opponent team has a very weak pass defense, certainly you would want to plan a strong passing offense. Put your best passer and receivers into the game. Select a series of pass plays and rigorously practice these in preparation for the game. Plan ahead and be prepared.

If you are planning to take a long automobile trip, very likely you will wisely use a map to mark your route from point to point. You may even set goals, sometimes called mileposts, as to where you want to be at the end of each day, making allowance for distances, weather and road conditions, visits and other stops you expect to make along the way. This is no different than preparing a strategy.

We make plans and establish strategies in our daily lives. We should do the same if we want to win at the game of poker. . .

> A strategy is a plan made in anticipation of a set of circumstances or conditions that can be expected to occur, with the objective of achieving certain well-defined goals.

Be prepared if you want to be a winner.
It "pays" to be prepared. . .

Developing the Poker Strategies for Winning

In the game of poker, there are a wide variety of conditions or situations that can arise. Many of these are more likely than others and can be expected to occur more frequently. Poker strategies simply take these conditions and situations into consideration in order to be prepared.

For example, we can ask ourselves what is the best thing to do if we hold such-and-such cards and an opponent is showing such-and-such in his upcards. When should we raise? And what do we do if the betting goes this way or that? What is the wisest action? And how should we take that action for maximum effectiveness?

The Poker Strategies for Winners take into consideration the most likely sets of conditions and situations we can expect to experience while playing seven-card stud poker. *(To a large extent, these can be applied to other games of poker.)* Since we are using a deck of cards of known and fixed content, there are finite probabilities of different events for every set of conditions -- although reasonable estimates are quite adequate for our purposes. With this information, it is possible to select the most advantageous plan of action in every case -- the one for which the odds are most in your favor.

Because there is, of course, the element of chance or luck -- for example, someone may draw the only remaining card to an inside straight and beat your three-of-a-kind, when he had no business staying in the pot -- there will be occasions when our strategies do not appear to work for us. But, in the long run, using the strategies will ensure that you will win more often -- and, very important, win more money ($) when you do win.

In presenting these Poker Strategies for Winners, it is desirable to provide a rationale in each case. It is important to fully understand the reasoning for each strategy in order to realize maximum effectiveness. Learning a strategy by rote is less likely to achieve its objective because there are bound to be subtle variations to be taken into account.

When you have a complete understanding of the strategy including the rationale, you are in a much better position to take the most favorable action and to make appropriate adjustments during the play of a hand -- and you don't have to be a genius to do so. . . Just learn the Poker Strategies and understand the rationale for each.

The Nine Key Poker Strategies

The following Poker Strategies are the most important because they represent situations that will be encountered very often while playing seven-card stud. *You can bet on it!*

A PokerShark will be intimately familiar with each strategy, and prepared to apply each without having to give it a second thought -- almost routinely. The next chapter will describe other strategies that are also important but occur less frequently or have less impact on the hand. We refer to these latter as Strategies for Special Situations.

All of these strategies relate primarily to seven-card stud. They may also be adapted and/or applied to other poker games. The Rules and Strategies for Texas hold'em will be discussed in Chapter 5.

A "hole" can be defined as a hollow place, or an opening into or through something. It's also defined as "a mean and dingy place" -- hardly a place for a good dealer to place any of your prized poker cards. A "hole" is also "an awkward position" in which to find oneself -- so why do we treat our "hole" cards with such reverence?
-- from "The Unusual Language of Poker" by George Epstein; *Poker Digest*, August 10, 2000.

RAISING ON AN OPENING PAIR

Basic Poker Rule #3 explained when you should stay in the hand with an opening pair. *(You might want to review that rule at this time.)* How should you <u>best</u> bet or play that hand. What is the best strategy?

For example, there may be some occasions when it would be wise to raise rather than just call the opening bet:

> • **If you are dealt a pair of aces, kings, queens or jacks, consider raising on third street.**
> • **If your pair is queens or jacks, consider raising only if no aces, kings, queens, or jacks (if you have a pair of jacks) show in the opponents' upcards and there has been no raise before you.**
> • **Make the raise provided either (1) there is at least the equivalent of three minimum bets in the pot when it is your turn to bet, or (2) it is a very loose table.**

Let's say you have been dealt two aces in the hole -- often called "pocket" aces. The chances are good that you will end up with two pair, aces-up. (There is also a good chance that you will not improve your hand, and end up with just

126

the pair of aces.) Aces-up is a fairly good hand and could be the winner. But, if too many opponents remain in the hand, it is quite likely that someone will draw a hand that beats you out.

After all, there are millions of possible poker hands in a 52-card deck, and the average winning hand is two pair, jacks-up. So, while your two pair, aces-up, is a bit better than the average winning hand, there are numerous hands that would make you second best. Coming in second in poker is costly, and we want to avoid doing so.

Starting with the highest pair on third street, you can expect to win more than 75 percent of the time if there is only one opponent in the hand against you. But that percentage drops to less than 60 percent if two other players stay in, and to about 30 percent if five opponents are still in the hand.

Therefore, the proper strategy in this case is to force out as many players as possible by raising the maximum amount allowed. By way of illustration, in a $1-to-$5 spread-limit game, assume the player with the low card on the board has made the mandatory minimum bring-in bet of $1.00. When it is your turn to bet, and you hold a pair of "pocket" aces (i.e., two aces in your downcards, hidden from the other players), you announce: "raise;" and place $6.00 in front of the pot. That's a $5.00 raise on top of the original bet of $1.00.

Winning is better than losing -- always. --Irene Epstein

127

Your objective in this case is to play "heads-up" against one player if possible. At the very least, you raise to reduce the number of active players in the hand -- so as to improve your chances of winning with only aces-up (or even only a pair of aces if your hand doesn't improve). The same strategy applies if you are holding a pair of kings, queens or jacks.

However, since your ultimate objective is to win money ($) -- as much as possible relative to the stakes -- it would make no sense to chase all the players out, leaving the pot with very little money in it. If you are playing in a Las Vegas casino poker room or elsewhere where there is no ante *(I refer to this as Las Vegas-type poker)* or in a very tight game, there should be at least three bets -- the forced bet by the low-card opener plus calls by two other players -- already in ahead of you before you make your raise. Otherwise there may not be any money in the pot when you win. Recognize that everyone may fold when you raise -- especially if you are seated at a very tight table; you want to win at least a few dollars.

If you hold a pair of aces and one of the aces is your upcard -- called a "split" pair of aces -- and hence in plain view, it is even more likely that all the opponents will fold when you raise. They likely will assume you have a pair of aces and wisely decide not to chase -- unless one holds a very strong starting hand. You can't win money if everyone folds when you raise, unless there already are some chips in the pot. This is all the more reason to make your raise only if there already is the equivalent of three or more bets in the pot when the betting round reaches you. Raising with a pair of "hidden" aces -- both aces concealed in the hole -- is less likely to chase everyone out of the hand. That is why concealed pairs have greater value than split pairs. (Another advantage is that your opponents are less likely to suspect you have made three-of-a-kind when a matching card is dealt to you face up.)

Of course, it is a different matter if it is a very loose game where there is a lot of betting and raising. Then you can make your raise when it is your turn to declare, expecting one or more opponents to call. You may even get a reraise! If you believe you hold the best hand (i.e., the raiser is not likely to have a higher pair or three-of-a-kind because at least one of his upcard is showing in the opponents' hands or, perhaps, is the same value as your "kicker"), you might reraise. That should really narrow the field while building the size of the pot!

In games where there is an ante, there is some money already in the pot before the cards are dealt. In that case, it may be prudent to make the raise when it is your turn to bet -- so long as there is the equivalent of three minimum bets in the pot. However, if the house has raked most of the chips from the antes, leaving less than the equivalent of three minimum bets, you would not want to make the raise at this point unless it is a very loose table.

If your upcard is low on the board -- and hence you are required to make the opening bet -- but you hold a pair of aces, kings, queens or jacks in the hole, you might elect to open for the maximum bet if the ante in the pot is the equivalent of three minimum bets. This will serve the same purpose as a raise and tend to reduce the number of opponents staying in the hand against you. *(I've seen players open for the maximum amount when they are low on the board without even looking at their hole cards. A PokerShark would never do that. . .)*

If you are dealt a pair of kings, you are fairly safe in making the raise if there are no aces showing in the opponents' upcards. Of course, it would be nice if all four aces were spread out, so that no one could possibly make a pair of aces against your pair of kings. (Note: A card higher in value than your pair, in this case an ace, is called an "overcard.")

If you are dealt a pair of queens, and none of your matching card (a queen) is exposed in the opponents' upcards, you are fairly safe in making the raise if there are no overcards (aces or kings) showing in the opponents' upcards. The same would apply if you observe three aces (or three kings) or, better yet, all four spread out on the board. But what if you see one or two aces or kings exposed? You have reason to hesitate. Chances are that he does not have the second ace (or king) in the hole. Your raise may force him to fold, thereby reducing the likelihood that he will catch a second ace or king on the next card; then your hand would become a poor second-best. So a raise in this case would be prudent, especially if the player is rather tight and likely to fold.

This same reasoning applies to a pair of jacks, except now there are more overcards to be concerned about.

After making that opening raise with your high pair, you may or may not want to make further raises on the subsequent rounds. If you have achieved your objective of reducing the number of players in the hand against you to one or two opponents, there is no reason to continue to bet or raise heavily unless you think that you hold the best hand and can build up the pot. If there are three or more opponents still in the hand, you might raise again (or bet the maximum allowed if you are high on the board or if they all check to you) in order to force out additional opponents. That, of course, depends on whether they are tight or loose players. A tight player is more likely to fold if you raise on fourth street. Raising against a loose player or an opponent who has a strong hand would be fruitless at this point, except to build up the pot. The question then is whether your hand still merits additional $ investment. *(See also Poker Strategy #4 on betting after the fourth card and Poker Strategy #5 on playing two-pair hands.)*

While we have recommended this opening raise strategy with a pair of queens or jacks, it is important to reemphasize the Basic Rule #3 that suggests you fold if one of your matching cards (queen or jack) is exposed in one of the opponents' upcards, unless you can get in very cheaply. So this strategy of raising with a high pair on third street should apply to queens or jacks only if none have shown up in the opponents' upcards. A possible exception would be if you are playing against very tight opponents who are likely to fold, leaving you heads-up against only one opponent. In that particular case, a raise mighr be appropriate.

But note that this strategy of raising on an opening pair on third street does apply when you are dealt a pair of aces or kings even if there is a match in an opponent's upcard, i.e., another ace or king.

An Important Exception to Poker Strategy #1

Having explained Poker Strategy #1, now consider an exception to it. In a structured-limit game, such as $2-$4 seven-card stud as played in many casinos, the opening bet is $1.00 minimum, $2.00 maximum. The low card on board is required to open the betting. Let's say that he opens for $1.00; several players call and it is now your turn to bet. You have been dealt a split pair of aces, one in the hole and one up. How should you respond?

Poker Strategy #1 calls for a raise in order to reduce the number of opponents -- based on the probability that you will end the hand with aces-up or just a pair of aces. But in this particular structured-limit poker game, only a $1.00 raise is allowed. That's the casino's rule for this game; and it may be the rule in other casinos too. Such a modest raise is not enough to force many players to fold, especially if they have already called the $1.00 opening bet — plus they have put up an ante so they feel they have an "investment" in the hand and will likely call your raise.

So, in such a case, it would not be prudent to make the raise because it probably will not chase many, if any, players out -- and it gives away information as to the strength of your hand. With an ace as your upcard, your raise is telling them that you have a pair of aces. On the other hand, if there were a lot of very tight players who are extremely conservative and likely to fold even with such a modest raise, it would, of course, be appropriate to make the raise. *(If the table had lots of tight players, you should have changed to another table anyway, because it is preferable to play against loose players or PokerPigeons.)*

On the other hand, if someone has raised just ahead of you, making the bet $2.00 total, you can then raise to make it $4.00 total ($2.00 call plus a $2.00 raise). If there are many players who have yet to bet, some of them may drop out because now it is relatively expensive to call the raise. Again, your objective in this situation is to reduce the number of players in the hand against you so as to improve your chances of winning with a high two pair or, if you do not improve, just the high pair.

This example illustrates why it is generally preferable to play at higher stakes than $2-$4 structured limit. The amount you can raise on third street is too small to force many opponents to fold. A $3-$6 structured-limit game is preferred in this regard because you can raise the opening bet to $3.00. Better yet, in a $1-$5 spread-limit game you can raise the opening bet to $6.00 (a $5 raise) -- enough to force out marginal hands and possibly some

133

hands that would have drawn to a small straight or flush if they had been allowed to stay in for $1.00.

Summary:

We can state the Poker Strategy #1, Raising on an Opening Pair, so as to accommodate most situations that are likely to arise during a game of seven-card stud poker:

• With a pair of aces or kings on third street, raise to reduce the number of opponents staying in the hand, provided there is at least the equivalent of three minimum bets already in the pot or there are a number of loose players at your table.

• With a pair of queens or jacks on the opening deal, raise if (1) your matching cards do not show up in the opponents' upcards; (2) you believe it would reduce the number of opponents staying in the hand; and (3) there is at least the equivalent of three minimum bets already in the pot or there are a number of loose players at your table who are likely to call your raise.

• However, it may not be wise to raise if the amount of the raise is so small that it would not likely force many players to fold -- unless there are a lot of very tight players at the table. Furthermore, raising gives your opponents information about the strength of your hand. (Higher stakes are preferred in this regard.) Make the raise if it will force out some of the opponents.

* * *

• POKER STRATEGY #2:

PLAYING WITH A MARGINAL OPENING HAND

We have already discussed marginal opening hands: You are dealt three cards that almost, but not quite, meet the criteria specified in Basic Poker Rule #3. And we have given several examples previously. Also, we have already indicated an appropriate strategy for such hands: Stay in on third street only if you can get in "cheap" -- for the minimum bring-in bet.

The rationale here is that you might improve your marginal hand on fourth street so that it becomes a hand that could ultimately win the pot. It is worth a relatively small investment to see what fourth street will bring you. If the hand does not improve, then you would, of course, fold if there is any betting on fourth street. But stay in if everyone checks, just in case. . .

For example, if you were dealt A♣ J♣ in the hole with the 9♠ up, this opening hand certainly has attractive possibilities: You could catch an ace for a pair of aces on fourth street; and you could catch another club for a chance to make an ace-high flush.

We use this example only as an illustration. Any combination of three cards in an opening hand that could develop into a potential winning hand depending on the next card dealt, meets this criteria. PokerPigeons stay in on too many of these marginal hands, and then often remain in the hand to the end. PokerSharks play very few of these hands; and, when they do stay in under the right circumstances, often fold on fourth street unless the hand has improved. *(See Strategy #4.)*

When to Stay In on Third Street
With a Marginal Opening Hand

Under no circumstances would a PokerShark call the opening bet with a marginal hand unless certain criteria are satisfied. Both of the following conditions <u>must</u> be met to warrant a decision to stay in and invest $ in this hand:

(1) The cards needed to make the hand attractive -- and worthy of further investment -- are live for the most part. Thus, in the above example where you were dealt A♣ J♣ in the hole with the 9♠ up, if an ace was showing among the other players' upcards, you should drop out. Likewise, if three or more clubs had fallen, you should also fold your cards; and,

(2) It only requires a minimum bet to call. If you are the last to bet and the opening (forced) bet is the minimum and it has not been raised, then your marginal holding is worth a call. On the other hand, if there are players to your left, yet to bet, who are likely to raise, it would be prudent to fold your marginal hand. If one player to your left is very aggressive and has been raising almost every hand, you can assume he will do the same again. (You really would like to be seated/positioned to the immediate left of such a player.). If there are opponents yet to bet

showing high cards, unless it is a very tight game, you can expect one to raise the bet -- making marginal hands unattractive.

It is strongly recommended that you understand and religiously apply this strategy for marginal opening hands. Otherwise, you will find yourself enmeshed in too many losing hands that will be costly. An unwise, improper investment in a marginal opening hand often results in a decision to see "one more card" -- and then perhaps yet another; meanwhile the bets get larger and the cost grows.

If you are playing in a no-ante game, there is even more motivation to fold marginal hands unless the potential is very great. After all, until you call the opening bet, it hasn't cost you a single penny.

Table position can make a difference. Let's say the opening bettor is to your right and makes the minimum bring-in bet; and now it your turn to declare. You have a marginal opening hand -- like A-K-9 unsuited -- with no aces or kings exposed in the opponents' upcards. These cards do not meet our criteria in Basic Poker Rule #3 but they do offer possibilities if an ace or king were to be dealt to you on fourth street. You would like to stay in and see. But there are players to your left yet to bet; almost certainly there will be a raise. You must fold your hand. Had you been last to declare (if the opening bettor had been to your immediate left) and the bet had not been raised, then you would be correct in calling the opening bet.

An Experiment

As an experiment during a visit to Las Vegas, I decided to play more marginal hands than I normally would. I did this for the first few days of my visit; and then, for the rest of my visit, I reverted to playing according to the Basic Poker Rules.

The first three days, I called with a low pair (sevens or lower) without a high kicker; I stayed in with a pair of jacks or queens when one was showing in an opponent's upcards; and I stayed in with two cards to a straight or flush so long as one of my cards was a high card (A, K, or Q). And I often stayed in on fourth street even if my hand did not improve.-- if I thought there was a chance to improve on 5th - 7th streets. The result: I lost more $ than I won, suffering a significant net loss for those three days. *(I also noted that, when I played these marginal hands, there was a tendency to "press my luck" in my desire to make up for the losses. Also, I wanted to play hands that were less than marginal; I resisted doing so.)*

Then I reverted to playing by the rules for the next two days. The first day, I played very few hands the first two hours. I was patient -- waiting for the right cards in accordance with Basic Poker Rule #3. Then the cards "turned" and I started getting good opening hands; most of those became winning hands. Fortunately my winnings the last two days made up for my losses the first three days.

———

A traveler without knowledge is like a bird without wings.
--Alan Spira, quoting a Muslim sage

A Quiz for You

Here's a little two-question quiz to test your under-standing of this strategy for playing marginal opening hands.

Question #1: You are dealt a pair of sixes in the hole and a king up. How do you play this hand?

Answer: It depends. . . Are there other sixes or a king showing? If so, you should fold. If not, you can play as long as you can get in for the minimum opening bring-in bet.

This is a hand I was actually dealt. I observed that there were no other sixes out, but two kings were showing in the opponents' upcards. (Furthermore, two players showed an ace as their upcards. That meant there was a reasonable chance one of them would make a pair of aces.) Of course, I folded this hand.

Question #2: You are dealt a split pair of jacks with a five as your kicker. There is one other jack showing in an opponent's upcard. How do you play this hand?

Answer: Stay in only if you can play with a minimum opening bet. If the pot is raised before it gets to you, or there is an aggressive player to your left showing a high card greater than a jack, you should fold.

* * *

If this is the best of all possible worlds,
what then are the others? -- Voltaire

- **POKER STRATEGY #3:**

STARTING WITH THREE-OF-A-KIND

Being dealt three-of-a-kind, sometimes referred to as "rolled up" or "triplets" or, more often, "trips" -- a pair in the hole with a matching third card face up -- is very exciting! There is a reasonable chance of making a full house -- even a chance of getting four-of-a-kind. *And that is really very exciting!* It's a great feeling when you look at your downcards and the upcard, and see rolled up aces; even rolled up deuces. . . Three-of-a-kind! Trips!

More likely, you won't improve this hand and will end up with the three-of-a-kind as your final hand.* But the trips are likely to win the pot anyway. And, if you do improve it, you will be holding a "monster hand." But these kind of hands are quite rare; so you want to make the most of them. How you play the hand can have a strong bearing on your winnings for a session.

Many good poker players will tell you not to bet or raise (i.e., check or call only) until fifth street. They reason, quite properly, that you want to build up the size of the pot because your chances of taking it are very good.

---

* If you start with three-of-a-kind, your hand will <u>not</u> improve 58.87 percent of the time. It will improve 41.13 percent of the time.
-- From "Seven-Card Stud: Ending Up Right Where You Began" by Mike Caro; *Card Player*, Jan. 27, 1995.

Of course, you do want to maximize your winnings. Keep in mind that raising (or even betting) on third and fourth streets could chase out many players, especially if you are playing at a tight table. It also gives your opponents who do not fold some valuable information: They now suspect you have a strong hand and will be more cautious in playing against you. As a consequence, they will be less inclined to call your bets/raises later in the hand, thereby preventing you from winning as much $ as you might have otherwise. To avoid this, it may be advisable to simply call the bet, depending on the value of your trips.

Only after the fifth card is dealt should you plan to raise with medium-to-high trips — unless you are playing at a very loose table.

Note that we have restricted this strategy recommendation to medium-to-high (eights or higher) three-of-a-kind opening hands, and have made an exception for games where there are a lot of loose players who would likely stay in even after you raise. The same might be said for a high stakes game if there already is a lot of money in the pot. In this case, even if all opponents were to fold, you would still be ahead a significant amount of $.

If an opponent raises on third street, your best move is simply to call the raised bet. Don't reraise, or else you will find too many opponents folding their cards. The same is true on fourth street.

141

What should you do if you are high on fourth street and must declare the opening bet for that round? You can check. We will refer to this as the "Call/Check Strategy." With trips, on third and fourth streets it is recommended that you call all bets but check if you are first to bet or if others before you have checked.

But there are cases when this Call/Check Strategy may not be the most advantageous. Much depends on the nature of the game and the players involved. If the game is tight and the opponent players are very conservative, the Call/Check Strategy certainly is the best. On the other hand, in a very loose game with lots of betting and raising, a minimum (or slightly higher, if allowed) bet would be warranted. You will get some calls; and increasing the size of the pot makes it easier to keep other players in the hand. That's what you want, especially if you fill up for a full house!

Suppose you held two aces in the hole, and, on fourth street, your upcards were A-K suited. Your opponents see the A-K suited. Under these circumstances, they likely would interpret a check as "sandbagging." They strongly suspect that you are checking with the intention of raising after someone bets. Suspecting this possibility would make them more cautious, and hence less likely to bet. But you want to build up the pot. So it might be advisable to make the minimum bet in such a case.

Whether or not to make a bet under these circumstances is really a matter of judgment; you are in a better position to make this decision if you understand how your opponents are likely to react, and then make your bet or check accordingly. The looser the game, the more likely they will call. If the table is fairly tight, a check is the only way to ensure you won't force out most of the opponents. When in doubt, don't bet; check instead.

Another Important Exception

On fourth street, you hold three-of-a-kind; an opponent's upcard shows your matching card, and your other card (the kicker) is matched by two or more of the other players' upcards. You cannot possibly make four-of-a-kind; and, your chances of filling up to make a full house are very poor. Most likely the three-of-a-kind will be your final (and best) hand. Therefore a strong bet or raise is recommended; your objective is to force out as many opponents as possible.

* * *

But raise on third street if your trips are low.

Up to this point, this strategy has been concerned only with middle-to-high trips. What if you should be dealt a low (sevens or lower) three-of-a-kind hand? In that case, a strong bet or raise should be considered. Now your objective is to force out as many opponents as possible -- especially those who may hold a higher pair with the potential of catching the third to make a higher three-of-a-kind hand

143

than you hold, or drawing to a straight or flush. By betting the maximum or raising at this point, you improve your chances of winning with a small three-of-a-kind hand.

* * *

Strategy Review: Starting With Three-of-a-Kind

This strategy is important, and so it is appropriate that we review it, including the exceptions discussed, with respect to two broad, typical situations that are quite likely to occur:

(1) Medium-to-High Three-of-a-Kind on Fourth Street

In general, the best strategy with a medium-to-high three-of-a-kind (eights or better), when you are high on fourth street -- and therefore must make the opening bet -- is to make the same bet you would have made if you held only a high pair on fourth street: Check. If anyone bets, you simply call -- do not raise. At this point, you want to keep as many opponents as possible in the hand because you likely hold the winning cards, and you want to maximize the amount of $ in the pot at the end.

With a medium-to-high three-of-a-kind, the time to raise is after the fifth card has been dealt. Our strategy here is intended to maximize the $ winnings. Had you raised on third or fourth street, you probably would have driven most, if not all, of your opponents out of the pot. By the fifth card, there are more likely to be opponents with hands worth playing further (that means more $ for you when you win); and, if by chance all of the opponents should fold at that point, there will be some money in the pot for you to win. But note the exception if your kicker and the matching cards are shown in the opponents' upcards; then it would be desirable for you to raise.

(2) Low Three-of-a-Kind on Fourth Street

Suppose that your three-of-a-kind is low, i.e., three sevens or lower. A low three-of-a-kind is really not a very strong hand. Certainly, it will win many pots but it can be beaten by a higher three-of-a-kind as well as a straight, flush, etc. Therefore it is advisable to play this hand the same way you would a high opening pair of aces or kings, and for the same reason: Bet the maximum or raise so as to reduce the number of active players in the hand against you.

* * *

How to Make the Bet/Raise on Fifth Street

When betting or raising with three-of-a-kind on fifth street, you want to take precautions not to provide information to your opponents by your mannerisms or facial expression. Calmly announce: "raise," as you put your chips in front of the pot. Then lean back and maintain a "poker face," showing no emotion or expression. Avoid eye contact with any of your opponents. Don't stare at any of them. Be calm and relaxed. Let your opponents decide how to respond without trying to influence their actions. *(There may be times when you will want to influence their actions, but this is not one.)*

A Short Quiz for You

You are playing in a $3-$6 structured-limit seven-card stud game, and are dealt rolled up queens — trips! An opponent showing the 3♦ makes the minimum bring-in bet of $1.00. Two others call, and then the player two seats to your right raises it to $3.00. He shows J♦ as his upcard. The player to your immediate right showing an ace up, calls. It is now your turn. How do you best respond?

Answer: Simply call. With three queens rolled up, you want to keep as many players as possible in the hand. If you were to raise, you would likely force out most of your opponents. At this point, you hold the best hand and are favored to take the pot. Wait till fifth street to raise so you can build as large a pot as possible.

* * *

Some Additional Interesting Statistics. . .

• In seven-card stud, if you are dealt a pair on third street, the odds are 13-to-1 against making a full house or four-of-a-kind. On sixth street, the odds against it will increase to 38-to-1.
• Starting with three-to-a-straight in sequence, the odds against getting the straight are 4-to-1.
• Starting with three-to-a-flush, the odds against making a flush are 4.5-to-1.
• However, if you have four-to-a-flush on fourth street, the chance of making the flush are about 1-to-1, even money.
• With four-to-a-straight in sequence on fourth street, the chance of making the straight are not quite as favorable: 3-to-2 against you.

• POKER STRATEGY #4:

BETTING AFTER THE FOURTH CARD

We have discussed previously (see the Basic Poker Rule #3) the appropriate holding cards to warrant an opening bet (i.e., staying in): pairs, three-of-a-kind, three-to-a-straight, and three-to-a-flush — with certain conditions in each case. Now the fourth card is dealt — fourth street, and you must decide whether to call, raise, or fold.

This is a very important decision point. If you make the wrong decision, it can become very costly. Should you decide to stay in, you will have made an initial investment and be inclined to remain in the hand as the game progresses — even with a marginal hand or one of questionable merit. And, what's more, as the hand progresses, the betting and raising generally get higher — more $; and raises are more likely on fifth through seventh streets.

> *The general principle here is that you must improve your hand on fourth street or have three-of-a-kind in order to stay in the hand — unless you can draw a card cheaply.*

Improving an opening pair means making three-of-a-kind or possibly two pair. Improving three-to-a-straight means being dealt a fourth card in the sequence and open at both ends. If you start with three-to-a-flush, improving it

147

on fourth street means drawing a fourth card to the flush you hope to make. In almost all of these cases, you should stay in the hand. However, with two pair, you <u>may</u> want to raise the pot -- or you may be well advised to drop out of the hand; we will discuss these alternatives and concomitant strategy below.

But our strategy must allow for exceptions. There may be times when you should fold even if you do improve your hand on fourth street.

By way of illustration, in a $1-$4 spread-limit game, I was low with a five up and was forced to open the betting on third street. I held a six and seven in the hole -- giving me a low three-to-a-straight in sequence (5-6-7 unsuited). Normally I would have gone out with such a low sequence unless I could get in with only a minimum bet; but, since I was low on the board, I was forced to start the betting. My next card was an eight. I now held four to an open-ended straight -- but I dropped out when an opponent made a bet that was more than the minimum. The reason: I observed two fours and two nines in my opponents' upcards. My chance of making the straight was poor, and the pot (or investment) odds were not favorable relative to the card odds. That is, the chance of making my hand was low compared to the amount of money that I would have to invest, considering the $ amount already in the pot. It would have been a poor investment for me to remain in that hand.

Another example of interest: I held three small-to-medium diamonds to open. My hand did not improve on fourth street, but I stayed in the hand on a check-all-around. The fifth card gave me a fourth diamond -- a small card, but not in any sequence. A player showing a pair on the board came out betting and was raised by another player showing A♥ K♥ J♥. I held four to a flush; but, nevertheless, I threw my cards in, dropping out of the hand. Rationale: The opponent showing the A♥ K♥ J♥ was just as likely as I was to make a flush, assuming he held a fourth ♥ in the hole; and, if so, his flush would easily beat mine. Also, the pot odds were quite low relative to the odds of making the flush. I would have had to invest $5.00 to try to win $25.00. That's pot odds of 5-to-1; whereas, my chances of catching the diamond flush were much poorer — card odds of about 8-to-1 against me — based on the number of unseen diamonds that might be available at that point in the game.

To reiterate Poker Strategy #4:

> *Allowing for a few exceptions, if you do not hold trips and you do no improve your hand on fourth street, you are generally wise to fold.*

Other Exceptions

In addition to the cases noted above, there are other exceptions to this strategy for betting on fourth street.

• Certainly if everyone checks, there is no reason to fold your cards.

• If you hold three-to-a-flush or three-to-a-straight, including high cards (ace, king, queen) and very few of these have fallen, and only a minimum call bet is required, it would be appropriate to stay in for another card. But be wary of the possible three-of-a-kind hidden in one of the opponents' hands; s/he may be slow-playing (sandbagging) to keep you in the pot. Should you improve your hand on the next card, be cautious of calling any heavy betting and raising on fifth street. Ask yourself the following two fundamental questions before calling.

(1) Does the heavy bettor/raiser likely have a hand that would beat me even if I were to make my hand? For example, if he is betting on what appears to be an A-K high flush, and your highest card to a flush is the queen and several of your suit have fallen, you may be wise to drop out rather than chase the flush.

(2) Is there enough money in the pot to justify a somewhat large investment that a call would require at this point -- relative to the chances of making this hand? For example, say there is $16.00 in the pot, and you would need to put in an additional $8.00 to call the raised bet. In this case, the pot odds are only

$$16 \div 8 = 2 \text{ (or 2-to-1)}$$

In other words, in order to win $16.00, you would have to invest $8 -- if you win. Not very attractive odds. . .

Consider the case if you have four-to-a-flush on fourth street with two more cards yet to be dealt, and there are three of your suit already exposed in the other players' upcards. Up to this point, your opponents have received 12 upcards; therefore, including your four cards, you have been able to see 16 cards. In all, 7 of your suit are accounted for (your four plus the three in the opponents' upcards); so there are now six remaining unseen (13 - 7) "flush cards" out of a total of 36 unseen cards (52 - 16) including your own hole cards, then the odds of making the flush are approximately

$$2 \times 6 \div 36 = 1/3$$

This calculation shows that the card odds are 3-to-1 against making the flush (the inverse of the above). Since the pot odds (2-to-1) are so much poorer compared to the card odds (3-to-1), this would not appear to be a prudent bet -- not a wise investment.

On the other hand, if there were several other players in the pot, and the pot contained (say) $40.00, then the pot odds for the same $8.00 call bet, would be 5-to-1, and the call would be the right thing to do -- unless you are quite certain that someone already has a higher hand than your flush-to-be-made.

If the pot odds are very close to the card odds, you might also want to consider the <u>investment odds</u>; i.e., an estimate of the amount of money you might <u>potentially</u> win relative to your total investment, should you make the flush, considering the odds of making the flush:

> Estimated Investment Odds =
> [Estimated $ that you might win ÷ Estimated $ you will have to invest] x Odds of winning

Investment odds greater than 1 are favorable. In such a case, it would be prudent to call the bet and stay in to be dealt the next card. For example, if you expect you might have to invest a total of $20.00 during the play of the hand, to win a pot containing $60.00 at the end, the odds of winning must be at least 1-to-3 to warrant a call on your part:

Investment Odds = ($60 ÷ $20) x 1/3 = 1

During the play of the hand, no one has the time or inclination -- even if he knows how -- to compute these various odds; so the best thing you can do is to have a "feel" for them. If there is very little money in the pot and only a few opponents still in the hand, the investment odds will not be attractive. You would probably be wise to fold -- unless you could stay in for a minimum bet or, better yet, if every one checked. However, if there are several opponents still in the hand and a significant size pot has already been built up, the pot odds and the investment odds would undoubtedly be favorable. In that case, assuming you have a decent chance of catching a card that would give you the winning hand, you should elect to stay in the hand.

When you are drawing to a straight or a flush, the more opponents staying in the hand, the better it is for you. It makes the investment odds more favorable. . .

Remember that bluffing is common in poker; a raised bet may be just that -- hoping to chase you out before you draw to the flush (and a winning hand). In such cases, it helps to know how your opponents play. Does the raiser frequently bluff? Is he overly aggressive by frequently raising? If so, you should be more inclined to stay in. On the other hand, if the raiser is a very tight player, he is less likely to be bluffing and greater caution is warranted. Carefully consider the investment odds.

Should you make your flush on sixth street, caution is still advisable. Other players may be holding hands that could beat your flush. For example, if the opponent with two pair catches the full house, your flush becomes a very poor second-best. Accordingly, in such a case where an opponent has a reasonable chance of making a full house, you would not want to raise the pot, but simply call the bet.

Don't raise if there is a reasonable chance that your opponent could have a better hand!

However, if most of the players have checked before you, then you should make the maximum bet because you probably have the best hand -- and a very good chance of winning -- so you want to get as much money as possible into the pot. You are trying to maximize the amount of your winnings.

* * *

A "hand" is a part of your body at the end of your arm, used for grasping and holding things. So why do you call the cards that are dealt to you a hand?
And, what's more, if you give a performer or speaker a hand, you are showing your approval of his/her performance or presentation; but we don't always approve of the cards that the dealer presents to us at the poker table.

-- from "The Unusual Language of Poker" by George Epstein;
Poker Digest, August 10, 2000.

• POKER STRATEGY #5:

PLAYING TWO-PAIR HANDS

What do you do when you make two pair on fourth street? You started with a pair and went in on the opening bet; now the fourth card dealt to you has paired your kicker so that you hold two pair. How do you BEST play this hand?

The Conservative Strategy

While two pair <u>may</u> take the pot, it is not a very strong hand; your chances of making a full house are not very good. At very best, if none of your needed cards shows up on the opponents' upcards, then there are, at most, just four cards in the deck that will help your hand. That's four out of all the cards that you have not observed. (<u>Note</u>: You have observed all of your opponents' upcards and all four of the cards dealt to you.) The odds of making a full house are about the same odds as drawing to an inside straight: poor.

With two pair, your chances of filling up to make a full house are not good. Let's say you get to seventh street with your two pair and there are one each -- two in all -- of your matching cards still in play. Assume that there are 14 upcards that have been dealt to your opponents at this point, plus the 6 cards you hold; i.e., there are 14 + 6 = 20 cards that you can observe. Therefore there are 32 cards (52 - 20) that contain the two remaining of your needed cards. Your chance of getting one of these is just 2 out of 32 -- a 6.25

percent chance. In other words, it is very unlikely that you will improve your hand -- 93.75 chances out of 100 that you will not make the full house versus only 6.25 chances out of 100 that you will be successful. At best, if all four of your needed cards were still live, the chance of improving your hand would be just 12.5 percent; that's steep odds against you of 7-to-1, not very good.

Some very conservative experts have suggested that you should fold in this situation unless you have aces-up; or, with kings-up, you should stay in only if three or more aces are spread around the table in your opponents' upcards and no one is betting strong or raising. Otherwise you are likely to find that you will lose more money by playing your two pair to the end than you will win when they hold up or (joy of joys!) you make the full house. Of course, you should always stay in if everyone checks.

Many experts disagree with this strategy for playing two-pair hands on fourth street, including myself. We might call this the Conservative Strategy for Playing Two-Pair Hands.

A new player might be wise to use this strategy, but should consider switching to a more aggressive strategy as he develops his poker skills.

A More Aggressive Strategy

I have developed a somewhat less restrictive, and hence less conservative strategy that can be used in this situation, which I prefer. Indeed, if the game has a significant ante, then this less conservative strategy is even more desirable. After all, two pair is a respectable hand and does win many a pot. But, if you want to play such a hand, then you must take steps to enhance your chances of winning, and you must be very cautious. It also helps considerably if you really know how your opponents play. *(Note: It cost me a lot of money to learn this strategy because I did not want to play according to the more conservative strategy. So be forewarned. . .)*

We will call this less conservative strategy

Epstein's More Aggressive Strategy for Playing Two-Pair Hands

As we will explain, the implementation of this strategy depends on your starting hand on third street.

• Starting with a Pair of Aces or Kings

If you open the hand with a pair of aces or kings, then pair up for two pair on fourth street, at this point your best action is to bet or raise the maximum. Try to reduce the number of players against you. The more hands there are in the pot, the more likely someone -- not you -- will make a straight, a flush, or a small three-of-a-kind. Then you would be second-best -- a big loser!

If the other players drop out when you make your big bet or raise, then you have made a small pot. That is certainly better than calling all the way and then losing to a small straight or three-of-a-kind on the river. That could be quite costly.

• Starting With a Pair of Queens or Jacks

Let's take the case where you had opened with a pair of queens or jacks and you stayed in because none of your matching cards were showing in any of your opponents' upcards. Then you made two pair on fourth street. Your betting strategy in this case is very important; you could easily lose, and it could be costly if your hand is second-best.

In this case, on fourth street, there are several possible situations to consider based on your hand, the exposed cards, the type of opponents, and your betting position.

• High Hand

If your hand is high on the board -- and hence you are the first to bet (i.e., there are no higher cards exposed) -- you should bet the maximum amount in order to reduce the number of players in the pot against you. *Make your bet aggressively, as will be explained in Poker Strategy # 7.*

• Second, Third, or Fourth to Declare

If you are near the beginning of the fourth-street betting sequence and the players before you all have checked, you have two choices: check or bet.

Observe whether there are any higher cards (overcards) exposed in your opponents' hands who have yet to declare (i.e., players to your left). That would be an ace or a king, or a queen if you have jacks-up. For example, if a player to your

157

left shows a king and none others are showing, he may be holding a pair of kings or have the potential of making kings-up -- a higher two pair than yours. In that case, you should be inclined to check. On the other hand, if you know that player to be very tight and likely to fold with a small pair, then a maximum bet would be in order.

However, if the higher cards exposed were all of the same rank and there were three or more of these showing, then you should bet the maximum. For example, let's say you hold queens-up. You observe three aces on the table and no kings. The chance of a two-pair hand higher than yours is very low -- about 1 chance in 34, or lower. Bet the maximum in this situation in order to force out some of your opponents and improve the probability of your two pair holding up through seventh street.

But if an opponent bets before you, you must carefully assess the situation. Why is he betting? If you think that he has a higher pair than you hold, it might be well to fold. If that player is very aggressive or loose and you think he is betting "on the come" (in anticipation of improving his hand), then you should call.

• One of Last to Declare

If you are seated in a position at the table so as to be one of the last to bet (but not necessarily the last), and all the players have checked before you, carefully consider the exposed upcards in your opponents' hands before making your decision:

If there are two or fewer overcards -- upcards higher in rank than the highest of your two pair -- you should make the maximum bet; again, this strategy is intended to reduce the number of players against you and chase out opponents who could draw higher hands. Hopefully, opponents with an ace or king (showing or hidden) will fold also, reducing the likelihood of a two-pair hand higher than yours.

Otherwise, if three or more higher cards are showing in the opponents' upcards but no more than two of each rank, you would be wise to check also. There is a good chance that one of them may hold or will make a higher two pair than you. If you were to bet and an opponent responded with a raise, you would be in trouble.

On the other hand, in a similar situation, if three or (better yet) all four aces were exposed -- no kings, or vice versa, then the probability of a higher two-pair hand would be minimal, and you would be wise to bet the maximum.

In this situation, if there has been only weak betting before it is your turn to declare -- and there is no raising, then you can call. In fact, it might be wise to raise! However, unless you are at a very loose table or playing against a very deceptive opponent, strong betting or raising by a Poker-Shark suggests that you drop out -- even with queens-up and no matching cards showing in the opponents' upcards. He could be sitting with a higher two pair or even three-of-a-kind. . .

To elaborate on this situation, suppose you hold two pair, queens and deuces, on fourth street. You look at the cards exposed on the table and observe two aces and two kings distributed among your opponents' upcards; and none of your matching cards are showing. There is a small bet of $2.00; several players call. Now it is your turn. By all means call the $2.00 bet; it is a small enough investment to have the opportunity to fill up on fifth street. The investment odds in this case would be very favorable. But also consider raising at this point if you think you can force out some opponents.

Assuming you only called this small bet, let's say that there is a raise by another player. You must respect the raise. Fold if he is a very tight player or a PokerShark. If you believe that player is loose, or deceptive, or prone to bluff or to raise "on the come" -- in the anticipation of improving a potentially strong hand -- you should call the raise, and check thereafter (unless you fill up, in which case you might want to sand-bag against the raiser). Likewise, if you know very little about the opponent, it would be wise to call his raise, just in case. . .

However, if you are convinced that the raiser -- a PokerShark -- has a better hand than you at that point, it would be prudent to fold your cards rather than invest further $ in that hand.

• Starting with a Pair of Eights, Nines, or Tens

If you are dealt a pair of eights, nines, or tens on third street, and then make two pair -- say, tens-up -- on fourth street, you do not have a very strong hand. As a matter of fact, it is a fairly weak hand. (*Since the average winning hand in seven-card stud is approximately three nines, a hand below jacks-up will win only about 15 percent of the time.*) If many players stay in the hand, your chances of winning are not good, and it can cost you dearly trying to make the full house. Yes, it is possible to win a decent size pot with tens-up, especially in a loose game; but that is the exception, not the rule. With tens-up on fourth street, you have three opportunities -- fifth, sixth and seventh streets -- to be dealt the card you need to fill up. That also means three rounds of betting, which could be quite costly. Your chances of filling up will not justify a potentially large investment. Let's consider the possible situations in this case:

• If two or more of your matching cards show in the opponents' upcards, you should drop out. Stay in only if everyone checks or you can "limp" in with a minimum bet.

• On the other hand, if only one (or none) of your matching cards shows in the opponents' upcards, you have three options depending on the circumstances:

(a) Drop out if there is strong betting or a raise, especially if it is a tight game and it is a tight player or PokerShark who is doing the betting/raising.

161

(b) You should call if there is only a minimum bet -- better yet if the cards are checked all around. (Always take that "free" card.)

(c) Bet the maximum if you are one of the last to bet and all of the players before you have checked. This bet is made in the hope of eliminating as many opponents as possible. But you should take this option only if there are no players yet to bet (to your left) who have up-cards higher in rank than your two pair. If you use this option, your most prudent action in subsequent betting is to check or just call (unless you happen to fill up); however, if there is strong betting or a raise, it would be wise to consider folding your cards.

- **Starting with a Pair of Sevens or Lower**

If you had gone into the hand with a small pair on third street, then you would have had to have held a high kicker-- ace, king, or queen. Thus, should you make two pair on fourth street, then the previous (above) recommendations would apply.

- **Responding to a Raise**

We have already discussed the situation when an opponent raises the pot on fourth street after you made your two pair. But if you are up against a PokerShark who is holding a high three-of-a-kind, he is likely not to raise you at that time. He is waiting for the next betting round

162

(as you would do under these circumstances). He is slow-playing to keep you in the pot. Consider this possibility.

The same applies if there is strong betting. Consider the probability of having the second-best hand. If that seems highly likely, fold rather than invest further $ in that hand.

It pays to know your opponents' playing styles in such cases. But, lacking that information, in responding to a raise, you must assume that your two pair is beaten and drop out <u>unless</u> your card odds are very high relative to the pot odds, and you are not likely to get caught between two raisers. (Most casinos allow three or possibly four raises on each round of betting. It could be very costly to get caught between two "warring" raisers, especially when you might be holding the second- or third-best hand.)

Of course you could be fortunate and make the full house on fifth street. What should you do if an opponent raises the betting? You should simply call the raise. Now <u>you</u> are slow-playing. A reraise would give your opponents' warning that you might have filled up. Some with potential straights or flushes would likely drop out. At this point, you want to keep as many players as possible in the pot. You can do your raising on sixth and seventh streets.

Of course, there is always the possibility that someone may have a higher full house than you. I once sat in a hand with three full houses. What a pot! So, if you are reraised, consider this possibility before you raise back again If you think the original raiser may have your full house beaten, you had better just call his reraise.

I once raised against a player with three sixes showing in his upcards; fortunately I had four nines -- well concealed! We raised and reraised until he ran out of money. I won!)

And then there was the time I made aces-full on the river, with two aces in the hole. I was up against one player who was apparently going for a diamond flush. He was high on the board, and came out betting. I raised; he reraised; I reraised; he reraised again!

Then I stopped to study his cards more carefully -- as I should have done before I first raised the bet. His three diamonds could be part of a straight flush, I realized. So I just called his last raise. Yes, he had caught the straight flush. My full house was second best; I lost that hand!

* * *

The harder you work, the luckier you get.
-- Gary Player, professional golfer

Character cannot be developed in ease and quiet.
Only through experience of trial and suffering can
the soul be strengthened, vision cleared,
ambition inspired, and success be achieved. -- Helen Keller

• POKER STRATEGY #6:

RAISING WITH TWO PAIR

There are times when it is prudent to raise with a two-pair hand in order to give yourself the best chance of winning.

Suppose that on the fourth card, you have made two pair; what do you do? Poker Strategy #5 (above) discussed the playing of such hands, and much of the following has already been covered. This strategy will supplement Poker Strategy #5.

If you choose to play using the Conservative Strategy for Playing Two-Pair Hands, then the following discussion would apply only if you held two pair with aces-up or kings-up. On the other hand, the following discussion on raising with two pair applies in all cases if you play according to *Epstein's More Aggressive Strategy for Playing Two-Pair Hands.*

Remember that you may want to fold your hand if there is strong betting or a raise, and several of your matching cards have already fallen and lie exposed in the other player's hands. Of course, even if several of your matching cards do show up, you would certainly stay in if everyone has checked.

In the event your matching cards are still "live," then generally you should stay in, hoping to fill up for a full house. But the chances of making a full house are quite small -- even if all your needed cards are live. Now then, two pair is a respectable hand and does win many pots -- so long as an opponent doesn't have a better hand. As previously noted, consider also that the more players in the hand, the less likely you are to win the pot -- and the more money it will cost you to stay in, especially if there is any significant betting or raising. Therefore, as noted in our discussion on Poker Strategy #5, the proper strategy in this case would be to raise the maximum in the hope of chasing out as many players as possible. *Please refer back to Strategy #5 for pertinent details.*

Remember that we are restricting this discussion to aces-up or kings-up if you play by the Conservative Strategy, but to all two-pair hands if you choose to use *Epstein's More Aggressive Strategy.*

Should you not fill up on subsequent rounds, you should simply call or check (i.e., do not raise again) -- unless you think there is a good chance of chasing out the remaining players by making a second raise. The more players staying in at that point, the less likely you are to force all of them out.

Should you be fortunate and make the full house, then hesitate before raising the pot on the next bet lest you chase out all the other players. If you have already made the BEST hand possible at the table, letting the others draw to flushes or straights is to your advantage. If one of them is so unfortunate as to make his flush, he will surely call

166

your final bet and may even give you an opportunity to raise. Betting position is critical in such cases, and good judgment is important too. If you are one of the last to bet, then a raise is in your best interests; you can only increase the size of your pot. If you have studied your opponents and know that they are loose and apt to chase, then a raise or strong bet in an early position may also be the right thing to do. Otherwise a modest bet or check (perhaps someone else will bet/raise) is appropriate; then you can reraise. (That's a good example of sandbagging -- and it's perfectly legal in most poker rooms.)

Note: An added benefit from raising is the "intimidation factor." Your opponents will be more leery of betting into you when they hold only moderately strong hands, in fear that you might raise. That can save you $ in the long run.

* * *

May all your days be royal.
-- Ginny L. Fahey; *Poker Digest*, July 29, 1999.

Never complain about your bad luck. Opponents won't be sympathetic. They'll be inspired. And they'll play better. Simply deny that you're experiencing bad luck. That's the road to profit. -- Mike Caro; *Card Player*, March 17, 2000.

• POKER STRATEGY #7:

PLAYING AGGRESSIVELY THE RIGHT WAY

To be a winning poker player, it is necessary sometimes to play aggressively -- but certainly not always. There is a time and a right way to play aggressively -- "selective aggression." If you can master this strategy, you will significantly enhance both your frequency of winning sessions and $ amounts won per session.

> • Play aggressively when it is to your advantage to do so.
> • Understand when and how to play aggressively.

Poker Strategy #1, Raising With an Opening Pair, is an example of when it is the right time for aggressive betting. You raise to force some opponents to fold their hands -- so as to increase your chances of winning. It also puts the remaining opponents on notice that you have a strong card holding, and issues a stern warning that they better have respect for you. At that point, you are in control of the hand -- so that you may be able to influence the course and style of betting. Opponents will have more fear of you and will be less likely to bluff against you; and they may hesitate to bet with medium-strong hands, even if they have the best hand. On the other hand, non-aggressive, passive players cannot control the game; they are simply along for the ride. *They strike no fear into their opponents.*

Your position at the table may suggest that aggressive betting would be to your advantage. Suppose you are seated between two opponents who are betting and raising. Both show potentially strong hands. You have a hand with a good chance of winning and would like to stay in, but this betting and raising and reraising is bound to get too costly for you when you are "caught in the middle." An appropriate aggressive action would be for you to raise the first bettor -- before the other opponent has an opportunity to do so. Now they respect you and are cautious in their betting and raising. You may even have earned a "free card" on subsequent betting rounds.

Indeed, in discussing the various Poker Strategies, we have often employed aggressive betting as part of the strategy -- a tactic to achieve the desired objective.

What is Selective Aggressive Betting?

Selective aggressive betting is making a bold bet or raise when your cards and the situation suggest this action would be to your advantage. It is going on the offense, attacking the "enemy" on the battlefield when it suits your cause, and doing so in a deliberate and forceful manner. At the poker table, it is betting when you might otherwise have checked; it is raising when you might otherwise have only called.

But it is more than just making a bet or raise; it is a style of betting with an impact. Make that bet with an air of authority and self-confidence. No hesitation. You know exactly what you are doing! Place your chips into the pot all at one time with a strong, firm, hand movement. *(This is something I learned from Mike Caro, the "Mad Genius of Poker," at one of his poker seminars at the Hollywood Park Casino.)*

We can liken the impact you want to achieve to the playing of Dvořák's Symphony No. 8 in G major. This symphony is an example of beautiful and exciting musical contrasts. In particular, the closing section, or coda, presents a whimsical, lilting waltz which suddenly changes gears into a rousing ending -- a dramatic outburst, closing in a blaring crescendo involving the entire orchestra.

This, after all, is the effect you want to achieve when you play poker aggressively. Make your opponents sit up and take notice! It's OK if they are frightened a bit. A dramatic change, whether it be in the music during the symphony or in your actions at the poker table, will accomplish that end. Indeed, proper and effective aggressive poker playing is just as beautiful to behold at the poker table as it is to hear the dramatic musical outburst in the finale of Dvořák's Symphony No. 8 in G major!

You want the opponents to "know" that you are very confident and comfortable in the action you are taking. This will make them respect you and your hand; it might even force a player with a marginal hand to fold. In fact, it could deliver the pot to you if all of your opponents drop out as a result of your strong, bold move.

Another reason for aggressive betting is to try to generate more $ in the pot, so as to build it up and maximize your winnings. This requires some judgment. If you chase all of the opponents out of the hand, you will not be able to build a pot. In other words, you must be discrete in selecting the best circumstances for aggressive betting.

Note: In discussing creativity in Chapter 6, "The Psychology of Poker," Dan Abrams points out that varying your style of play will make it difficult for your opponents to "read" your hands. You become less predictable. That is to your advantage, of course. Therefore, you are advised not to play aggressively at every opportunity or you will fail to confuse the "enemy."

The Key Criteria

For betting rounds prior to seventh street (see also *Strategy for Betting on the River* in Chapter 4), there are two rather broad criteria for determining whether or not to bet/raise aggressively:

> **Criterion No. 1 —**
> • **If your cards are high on the board and hence you are the first to declare, you should bet — rather than check — if you would call a raised bet (with a few exceptions).**

Having stated this criterion advocating an aggressive bet when you are first to declare because your hand is high on the board, there are times when it would <u>not</u> be prudent to bet aggressively. One such exception is when you hold medium-to-high trips on third or fourth street, as discussed in Poker Strategy #3. Another important exception would be when you have a marginal hand and would call only if you could get in cheaply -- i.e., a minimum bet or perhaps slightly more. A third exception is when your hand might merit a call but not a raised bet, and you suspect one of the opponents is likely to raise. In such cases, checking is the best course of action as opposed to aggressive betting.

Criterion No. 2 --
• **If you are in a late position at the table -- one of the last to declare -- and you hold a strong hand, then you should bet or raise aggressively if you believe that you have the best hand on the table (with a few exceptions).**

Note that we have restricted this tactic to late board positions and you are holding a strong hand. On the other hand, with the same cards, if you were seated in an early position with respect to the betting round, it would not be prudent to raise aggressively because a raise is likely to force out the weaker hands, while those opponents holding stronger hands would stay in and not fold -- definitely not to your advantage.

Again, exceptions in this case would be if you held medium-to-high trips on third or fourth streets, or had a good chance of connecting with a straight or flush. You do not want to raise too early and chase out any opponents *(see Poker Strategy #3)* when you may already have the winning hand or a very good chance to catch it. (Of course, on fifth street and, especially sixth and seventh streets, aggressive betting with medium-to-high trips would be highly desirable in order to build up the size of the pot.)

* * *

Yes, it always pays to be prepared. . .

Poker and Life --
Like in poker, a good portion of winning in life is simply good luck. I guess I've had my share -- both ways. Who hasn't? In the end, the "house" wins and the "chips" you've held for a little while are worthless. The "score" might be remembered for awhile by a few, but that too fades after a generation or two. "What's it all about?" I wish I knew. Meanwhile I play the hands that are dealt to me the best way I know how. Next time around, I'll try to do it better.
   -- Stuart Simon (entrepreneur/poker player) and Shirley MacLaine (actress)

• POKER STRATEGY #8:

PLAYING AGAINST AGGRESSIVE OPPONENTS

Aggressive opponents can be either tight players -- generally PokerSharks; or they can be loose players -- generally PokerPigeons. *(If there are too many PokerSharks at your table, you should have changed to another table long before this.)* But often there will be some of each. Be prepared. . .

Non-aggressive, often called "passive," players may also be tight or loose, depending on how conservatively they play their hands. A loose-passive player will stay in and call -- and call, but rarely take the initiative to bet; he is not likely to raise -- a perfect PokerPigeon. A tight-passive player -- sometimes called a "rock" for metaphorical reasons -- will play only strong hands, and is a threat only when he stays in beyond fourth street. Rarely will he raise the bet. (One practical problem, of course, is knowing a priori who are the loose-passive players and who are the tight-passive players at your table; it takes a while to make that determination by carefully observing how they play their hands.)

Strategy #8 is primarily concerned with aggressive opponents; they represent a much greater threat and challenge than do passive players. A tight-aggressive player is to be feared; he bets and raises only with a very strong hand. But, at least the tight-aggressive player is predictable (once you have properly assessed him). On the other hand, the loose-aggressive player is almost unpredictable; he may bet and raise almost with abandon, perhaps only based on the whim of the moment. *(In the long run, these too should be your PokerPigeons.)*

It's great for you if the aggressive bettor is a Poker-Pigeon -- sometimes called a *maniac* (one who craves the action). Preferably, you want to be seated just to the left of such a player, so he will declare before it is your turn. So long as you have a good playing hand, just go along with him and call his bets and raises. Even if you have the best hand at the table, in your opinion, don't raise against the loose-aggressive player until seventh street -- unless you want to protect your two pair or small trips. Let him build the pot for you. This strategy also avoids giving away information about your hand.

When a tight player is aggressive, be cautious. He may have a very strong hand. Do not deviate from the Basic Poker Rules. When faced with a raise or reraise, consider the pot odds relative to your card odds. Fold if the odds are not in your favor. Of course, if you hold a "made" hand or one with a good possibility of taking the pot, don't let the aggressive player force you out. It is possible that the PokerShark is trying to bluff you out. Certainly, if your hand is weak and the odds are not favorable, let him have the pot before you invest more $ in it.

* * *

A dollar saved is much more than a dollar earned.
You don't have to pay income taxes on the $ saved.
-- George Epstein

• POKER STRATEGY #9:

BLUFFING STRATEGY

A bluff is a form of deception. Usually it is an attempt to represent a weak hand as being a strong one -- the best hand in the game, in the hope of inducing your opponents to drop out of the hand so you can take the pot. *(Although, checking with a very strong hand also is a form of bluffing, sometimes called "reverse bluffing," the strategy we are discussing here is primarily concerned with bluffing to encourage your opponents to fold their cards.)* There is no doubt that pulling off a bluff or contending with your opponents' attempted bluffs are extremely important aspects of the game of poker. Expertise in this area is essential to being a winning poker player -- a PokerShark. It can easily be the difference between a winning and a losing session. . .

Bluffs involve betting. The bluffer can be the initial bettor or a raiser. Some poker experts believe that a check-raise is the most effective type of bluff. *(I know of no statistics on ths ploy, but a check-raise certainly is very dramatic and will strike fear into the hearts of many opponents.)* Also, a check-raise gives the bluffer an opportunity to assess the opposition based on their exposed cards, betting pattern, and response during that betting round. If the check-raise bluffer senses that the remaining opponents have weak hands, he is in a better position to carry forth with a successful bluff.

In pulling off a bluff, unless you are very good at it, some poker experts suggest that the best bluffing strategy is: *Don't Bluff!* If you are not skilled at it and try to bluff often -- and usually get caught, your opponents will be expecting the bluff and are more likely to call. In that case, you are likely to lose more money (when you are caught frequently) than you win (on the few occasions that your bluff succeeds).

PokerSharks know how and when to bluff. Some are prone to bluff often, early in the game, and continue to do so until an opponent calls the bluff and takes the pot. Thenceforth he will be more cautious and discriminating in selecting the bluffing opportunities while playing at that table. Another approach is to play tight for a while and then attempt to bluff. *(I prefer this approach.)* Based on their image of you, your opponents will treat you as a tight player and not suspect that you are bluffing, You can then continue to bluff more often -- until you are caught.

For the beginning poker player, once you learn this strategy, it is prudent to attempt to bluff occasionally -- hopefully, properly planned and executed. In fact, every PokerShark will bluff on occasion -- some more frequently than others. As a rough estimate, perhaps an average of one or two bluffs per hour of play would be reasonable. If there is a lot of player turnover at the table, somewhat more frequent bluffing may be warranted. But bear in mind, the lower the limit of a game, the more likely it is that a bluff will be called. It also helps to have a large stack of chips in front of you. This tends to intimidate your opponents and make them more respectful of you and, concomitantly, more inclined to fold when you bluff. On the other hand, never try to bluff out a player who is about to go all in.

Every bluff will not succeed. Once you get caught in a bluff, it is wise not to bluff again for a while -- unless there is a special circumstance or opportunity.

However, do let your opponents know that you got caught in an attempted bluff. This is called "advertising." They now know that you do bluff. Hence, they are more likely to stay in when you subsequently raise with a well-hidden "monster" hand -- thinking that you may be trying to bluff again. Thus, the attempted bluff will have had some value, after all. The threat of a bluff enables a player with a strong hand to win more $ than he would if the opponents knew that he never bluffed.*

The Stakes Make a Difference

The level of the stakes for the game is important. The higher the stakes and, therefore, the higher the cost to call a bluff, the more likely it is to succeed. In a $1-$2 limit game, where it only costs $2.00 to call a bet on seventh street, there are likely to be many more callers than if the bet were significantly higher -- say $6.00 or more. *(In fact, I do not recommend low stakes games below $3-$6 structured-limit or $1-$5 spread-limit for that very reason.)*

---

* "Bluffing -- Part II" by Lou Krieger; *Card Player*;
March 17, 2000.

178

How to Make a Bluff

There is a "right" time (opportunity) and a "right" way to make a bluff -- if you want to be successful. The idea, of course, is to be very convincing. You want your opponents to believe that you have the best hand; the less doubt in their minds, the better.

Among other factors, a successful bluff depends both on the way you develop and finally make the bluff, and the skills of the opponents you want to bluff out of the hand.

Try to assess your opponents as to whether they are loose or tight players. The tighter the player, the easier it will be to pull off your bluff.

Loose players are very difficult to bluff out; bluffs against such players generally should be avoided. Certainly, don't try to bluff out someone who is a veritable "calling station."* (*It may be my imagination, but it seems that elderly ladies are very tough to bluff out. They seem to be able to read my mind.*)

Opponents who bluff frequently are more likely to call your bluff -- so you should hesitate before deciding to bluff against such an opponent.

---

* "Six Keys to Becoming a Better Poker Player" by Lou Krieger; *Card Player*; July 11, 1997.

As an example of an appropriate bluffing opportunity, suppose your board shows four high clubs as your upcards on sixth street -- none in the hole *(but only you know that)*. The other players will likely "take" you for a flush if you come out betting. Therefore, if none of the other players is showing a strong hand, a maximum bet by you would be advantageous in this case -- especially if none are "calling stations." If they all fold their cards, you have won the pot. Even if one or more do stay in, you may make your flush on the river. This is called a "semibluff" -- bluffing with a hand that could improve on the draw. Furthermore, in making this bluff on sixth street, you are setting the stage for the next step in your bluff -- on the river.

At that point, a good bluffing strategy depends on the number of players still in the hand, their poker skills, and the size of the bet to be made. It is difficult to pull off a bluff against more than two opponents. It's much easier to bluff a single opponent. However, if the game is tight and most of the remaining players are PokerSharks, it could work for you. Bet the maximum without looking at your last downcard. *(Otherwise, you should <u>always look at all of your cards</u>, including the downcards, before betting or checking. The more information you have and the more accurate it is, the better it is for you.)* A tight player will only call if he has a strong hand; if he has a medium-strong or weak hand, your bluff most likely will succeed.

In anticipation of your bet on the river, one helpful tactic is to pick up some chips and jingle them in your hand while the dealer is dealing the last card down. An opponent, perhaps even a PokerShark, who has a "broken" straight or flush is likely to drop out, even if he has a pair, believing that you have a club flush. A PokerPigeon might fold even with a small-to-medium two pair. You win!

Note that, in this particular case, you "developed" your bluff by a series of planned actions: You bet the maximum when you caught the fourth club on sixth street; then you followed up with an unhesitating maximum bet as the last card was being dealt — even before looking at the last downcard. *(You were so confident!)* And, to further "convince" your opponent, you picked up some of your chips and jingled them in your hand — sort of a "reverse tell." *(You want him to believe that you are anxious to bet because you hold the high hand you are representing.)*

Hopefully, your opponent will be convinced that you do have the flush, while he did not make the hand for which he had been drawing. A really good player — a PokerShark — might call your bet because you do not have his hand beaten on the table; but a PokerPigeon would be so discouraged that he might literally throw his hand into the muck in total disgust.

If you are successful in a bluff, do not turn up your hand and show your cards. It is better to keep your opponents' guessing.

If an opponent asks about your hand as you rake in the pot, simply smile; make no verbal response. You are not obligated to reveal your hand. Pay no further attention to the requester; stack up your winning chips and prepare for the next hand. *(It feels so good!)* Alternatively, if you would feel more comfortable responding to a direct question, you can respond with a slight smile: *"Well, what do you think?"*

In the above example, we used the jingling of the chips as a device (or tactic) to help the bluff succeed. Other devices can be used. For example, a PokerShark who is trying to bluff with a "broken" straight on seventh street, might softly count out, while visibly moving his lips as he examines his downcards and upcards: "6-7-8-9-10." This device is quite effective. A rather subtle psychological tactic is to throw in a large-denomination chip when you make your bluffing bet, rather than smaller-denomination chips. Indeed, it is suggested that you do anything reasonable that could make your opponents believe that you hold the hand that you are representing.*

Bluffing on the River

As noted above, bluffing should be attempted infrequently. But there may be good opportunities to "steal" a pot on the river when you know that you are holding the second-best hand. In this case, your opponent has your hand beaten on the table, but you may be able to take the pot anyway by bluffing.

To illustrate such a situation, consider the following hand that I held while playing in a $3-$6 structured-limit seven-card stud game at Hollywood Park Casino.

---

* "Jingling Your Chips: Yet Another Strategy for Successful Bluffing" by George Epstein; *Poker Digest*; March 9, 2000.

My first four cards -- the two downcards in the hole and the first two upcards -- were all clubs. Only two other clubs had fallen in the opponents' upcards. So I had a good chance of making the flush; naturally, I decided to go for it. The player to my left showed a pair of kings in his upcards on fourth street. He bet the maximum ($6.00 in this game) and, of course, I called. As the game progressed, I made a pair of queens in my upcards -- but I did not make the flush. All I had was a pair of queens.

On the last round of betting, three of us remained in the game. The player with the pair of kings which was high on the board, checked to another player who showed four to a straight and three to a flush. That player, apparently unable to beat the pair of kings, quickly turned his cards over and dropped out of the game. That made life a lot easier for me, of course, leaving only the pair of kings with which to contend.

From observing this opponent's prior play, I knew that he was a "tight" player. Yes, he had me beaten; but I had been calling his bets all along and so he might figure that I held at least another pair in addition to the two queens showing in my upcards. He would likely "take" my hand for two pair, queens-up. This could be a good opportunity to try to pull off a bluff.

I considered the possibilities: One other king had fallen in another player's upcards, so it was unlikely that he had three kings. It was quite possible that he had two pair. But if he held just the pair of kings, then he might drop out if I bet. There was a good size pot at this point. And -- very important -- I knew that he was a tight player; and he was not deceptive. It was worth a $6.00 "investment" to make the bet in the hope that he only had the pair of kings, and would figure me for two pair or better. When I boldly made the bet -- without hesitating, he promptly threw his cards in. I had won a very nice pot even though I knew I was beaten on the board!

The Economics of Bluffing

At the start of this discussion on Bluffing Strategy, we suggested you should not try to bluff if you are not adept at it. If you have mastered this discussion and understand the key factors involved in making a bluff, then it can be a very profitable strategy for you. Don't be afraid to make an <u>occasional</u> bluff -- perhaps once an hour or so -- when the circumstances are proper (as just described above). The economics make it a sound investment. As you become more skilled in the "art" of bluffing, consider making more frequent bluffs.

Bluffing can be a very profitable investment; the payoff can be quite large relative to the amount invested.

Explanation:

Assume you are playing in a $3-$6 structured-limit seven-card stud game. By the time you reach the river, there could easily be $60.00 or more in the pot. Let's say that you have played your hand well and developed the opportunity to bluff; and you have decided to attempt it. You are high on the board, and come out betting $6.00, the maximum allowed in this game. If an opponent calls, and his hand beats you, it has cost you $6.00 to try to take the pot on the bluff. Note, however, that you only need to win just once out of ten bluff attempts to break even, assuming there is $60.00 in the pot each time. If, on the average, your bluffs succeed two or more times out of ten attempts, you will be well ahead.

A proper bluff can be a sound and poten-
tially quite profitable investment.

What If Your Attempted Bluff is Called or Raised?

There will be occasions when another player calls your attempted bluff. Assuming his hand beats yours, the only thing you can -- and should -- do is to turn over your hand, exposing all of your cards, and say: "Well I tried to bluff. You win." Yes, you have lost the pot but still gain some "advertising" value.

If an opponent raises when you attempt your bluff, it is <u>almost</u> certain that he has you beaten. Unless your river card brought you a big hand, generally it would be prudent to save another bet and fold. However, since the pot will be relatively large at this point, <u>it is wise to call if your hand is higher than the raiser's upcards.</u> Sometimes a devious player will suspect that you are bluffing and he will attempt to take the pot with a mediocre hand by raising. However, if another opponent calls the raise before you, chances are that player has your hand beaten and you would be wise to fold your cards.

How to Contend With an Opponent's Bluff

There will be many times when an opponent attempts to bluff you out of the pot. He has a powerful hand on the board, and has been betting "like he has it." The betting has been very aggressive.

If it is early in the hand -- on or before fifth street, you should be inclined to fold -- before you are heavily invested -- unless your hand is strong or has great potential. In that case, you should not be intimidated by the aggressive betting; by all means, call if the investment is merited.

If you are still in the hand on sixth street because you hold a strong/potential hand, the pot odds need to be assessed relative to the amount of money you will have to invest to stay in the hand and see, at least, the next card. A $6.00 call is not a bad investment if you think you have a reasonable chance of winning a $60.00 pot; i.e., card odds of less than 10-to-1 against you versus pot odds of 10-to-1 ($60.00 divided by $6.00).

Of course, if most of the cards you need to make your hand have already fallen in the other players' upcards, you would not have a reasonable chance of winning; the card odds are not favorable (greater than 10-to-1 against you). In that case, with the card odds higher than the pot odds, your best option is to fold.

On the other hand, when you get to the river and are still in the game for the final round of betting, no matter how your opponent has been betting, you should call if your hand is higher than his upcards. At that point, unless the pot odds should happen to be very low -- e.g., a $6.00 bet with only $12.00 in the pot -- a call is warranted. And, if your opponent has been bluffing, you would take the pot. **On the river, call him if you can beat a bluff!**

For example, suppose you have two pair and your opponent has four to a straight on the board. He bet on sixth street. You called. Now he again bets on seventh street. Perhaps he is bluffing; perhaps not. (Of course, if you had observed that most of the cards he needed to make the straight had already fallen in the other players' upcards, you could feel quite confident -- but not certain -- that you would win this pot.) You can look for "tells;" but, in any case, it is wise to call the bet because your two pair is higher than his upcards.

The same would be true if your opponent showed a pair of kings on the board. Should he have a second pair, you would lose. But the fact that your two pair beats his pair of kings strongly suggests that a call bet would be in your best interests -- just in case. . .

Let's put this strategy on contending with an opponent's possible bluff into somewhat greater perspective from a strictly economics standpoint: As long as you win when you call on the river, say, more than one time out of ten, you will be ahead. The amount of $ you win when you call his bluff will more than offset the amount you "invest" by calling and losing the other times.

> Always call on the river if your hand beats your opponent's upcards and the pot odds are favorable relative to the card odds.

The more often a player bluffs, the more inclined you should be to call when he bets. But don't raise unless you have a very strong hand -- preferably the nuts. You can not be certain that he is bluffing just because he does it often. If he were trying to pull off a bluff, then he would probably fold and your raise would gain you naught. However, if he were not bluffing and, in fact, held a strong hand, then you likely would be faced with a reraise by a hand that can beat your cards -- unless you hold the nuts.

* * *

The Difference between a Winner and a Loser -- *Anon.*

- A winner says, "Let's find out;"
  a loser says, "Nobody knows."
- A winner makes commitments; a loser makes promises.
- A winner says, "I'm good, but not as good as I ought to be;
  a loser says, "I'm not as bad as a lot of other people."
- A winner credits his "good luck" for winning -- even though
  it wasn't his good luck; a loser blames his "bad luck" for
  losing -- even though it wasn't his bad luck.
- A winner listens; a loser just waits until it is his turn to talk.
- A winner respects those who are superior to him and tries to
  learn from them; a loser resents the superiority of others
  and tries to find chinks in their armor.
- A winner does more than his job;
  a loser says, "I only work here."
- A winner says, "I fell;"
  a loser says, "Somebody pushed me."

CHAPTER FOUR -- POKER STRATEGIES FOR SPECIAL SITUATIONS

While the previous strategies are regarded as the most important because the situations involved are more frequently encountered, there are a number of other situations that will also arise. These too require pre-planned strategies to best handle each. In fact, it might be argued that some of these are just as important as those presented in Chapter Three.

The following poker strategies will be discussed in this chapter:

- Observing Your Neighbor's Hole Cards
- Using "Tells"
- Strategy on Card-Tracking
- Strategy for Betting on the River
- Raising With the Best Hand on the River
- Drinking While Playing Poker; Your Mental and Physical State

• <u>OBSERVING YOUR NEIGHBOR'S HOLE CARDS</u>

This strategy certainly has moral implications, but then too gambling also goes against many persons' ethical standards. I recall an occasion when several residents of a large apartment complex wanted me to present a seminar on poker. However the resident manager responsible for group activities, would not permit the seminar because, as he stated, "poker is a form of gambling," and he was very much opposed to gambling.

Likewise, I realize that many poker players will disagree with this particular strategy based on one's sense of right and wrong. Therefore I leave it to each individual to apply his own moral standards in this case. If observing your neighbor's hole cards -- due solely to his own carelessness -- disturbs your sense of right and wrong, I would suggest you skip this particular strategy.

Many poker players have a sense of ethics that forces them to close their eyes or look the other way when an opponent exposes his down (hole) cards. *Don't look the other way!* Should you have the opportunity to observe your neighbor's hole cards, be thankful because it gives you valuable information that places you at a distinct advantage. It is not cheating to take advantage of careless card-handling by an opponent sitting next to you at the table. (Don't strain your neck to peek at your neighbor's hole cards; that would be cheating.)

Suppose you have a pair of sixes with a king as the kicker, and there are no other sixes showing in the other players' upcards. Then the player to your right carelessly looks at his hole cards in such a way as to expose them to

190

your view. He has another six. With that bit of intelligence, you now know that your chance of making three sixes has been reduced to one-half of what you would have assumed without that information. So you quietly fold your cards, content in the knowledge that you have saved yourself the cost of at least one bet; and you wait for the next hand.

Suppose your careless neighbor reveals two clubs in his hole cards. As the game progresses, he catches three more clubs in his upcards. . . You know that he has a club flush, and now you can act accordingly when evaluating your own hand. For example, if you have made a straight, you can save a lot of money by dropping out at that point -- otherwise you would have to call his bet/raise.

It is even possible that a player across the table from you will expose a downcard during the game. It may be while folding his hand, or even during the play.

Exposing one's hole cards is careless card-handling. Certainly it is something you want to avoid. How a player sits at the table can be significant in this regard. A player who leans over the table with his torso extended well over the railing is more likely to expose his downcards. The corollary, of course, is that you should avoid sitting in this fashion. By all means, seat yourself comfortably, keeping your torso upright and essentially perpendicular to the table surface. Keep your hands cupped over your hole cards as you examine them. Avoid looking at your hole cards unnecessarily. Try to look at them once when they are first dealt to you, and then remember them. (But if you are not absolutely certain, by all means take another peek when appropriate.)

It needs to be reiterated that you should not play at a poker table or seat where the lighting is poor. If you have trouble reading your cards, you are at a big disadvantage. Too many hands are played incorrectly because the player <u>thought</u> he had a different card in the hole.

* * *

One should always play fairly
-- when one has the winning cards.
  -- from *An Ideal Husband* by Oscar Wilde

• USING "TELLS"

Many poker players, even experienced and skilled players, display mannerisms or characteristics depending on their cards. These are "tells." Look for them. They can provide you with valuable information. By getting to know your opponents at the table, you are in a better position to make important decisions based on their tells. In all cases, the tells should be interpreted and utilized based on all of the other information available. A tell should augment this information and never be the sole basis for making an important decision.

A tell is a player's physical or emotional response to the cards dealt. It is a reaction.

This phenomenon is analogous to the Third Law of Motion formulated by Sir Isaac Newton, the famed English physicist/scientist:
Every action is accompanied by an equal and opposite reaction.

Many tells are quite easy to discern, but their true meaning may not be apparent unless you carefully observe the player as the game is played, and correlate his play with the tell. In general, it is best to study one player at a time during each hand.

We will give a number of examples and explain their significance, but there may be many other tells. Look for them. . .

Tells can be classified:
- Involuntary Tells
- Voluntary (or Controlled) Tells

A third category are those tells that may be one or the other of these, depending on how deceptive is the perpetrator. We can refer to these as "Inconclusive Tells."

The Involuntary Tells are by far the most important. Here the player is giving you information without realizing it; this is information on which you can probably rely -- and play your hand accordingly.

On the other hand, Voluntary Tells are more likely to be feigned; the player is trying to deceive you. There may be steps you can take in this event to decide which type it is. Generally those that could be either involuntary or voluntary -- the Inconclusive Tells -- can only confuse you and must be disregarded unless you can test for their validity.

Examples of Tells

We will consider a typical situation to explain the various tells and the likely meaning of each. A player draws his last downcard (on the river) and looks at it. Watch him as he examines that card; see what he does.

One or more of the following reactions may occur which can give you a strong clue as to whether he has a good hand or is bluffing:

Involuntary Tells When Hand Has Improved --

• Eyes open wide;   Pupils dilate;

• Heavy/rapid breathing
(observe player's chest/diaphragm movement);

• Hand begins to shake;

• Glances quickly at his chips;

• Sits erect;   Straightens up in his chair;
Eagerly looks around the table;   Becomes alert
(as if preparing to go into action).

With these tells, the chances are that he has caught the card that makes the hand. The shaking hand may be the most significant of these, and you should look for it; but they are all worthy of note.

Each of these acts is a separate tell. If a player exhibits more than one at the same time, it serves to reinforce the message that he is (inadvertently) "telling" you if you are alert enough to get the message.   These Involuntary Tells inform you that your opponent has improved his hand. (You had better have a very strong hand in order to call.)

Then there are a number of Involuntary Tells that can indicate when an opponent is trying to pull off a bluff. These reactions are different than those when the hand has improved.   Observing these can make a big difference in whether you win or lose and how much $; so it pays to be aware and look for these during the game:

<u>Involuntary Tells When Bluffing</u> --

• Sudden perspiration *(uses handkerchief to wipe forehead);*

• Dryness of the mouth *(takes a long drink of beverage);*

• Nervous (uncontrolled) motions such as eye twitching, shuffling feet, and squirming in seat;

• Puffing deeply on cigarette *(if foolish enough to be smoking, and allowed to do so at the table);*

• Not looking directly at any of the other players *(a subconscious guilt feeling);*

• Licking lips *(perhaps warming to the "attack" or savoring the moment of anticipated triumph).*

If an opponent displays one or more of these mannerisms, the chances are he is bluffing. Take this into account along with all the other information you already have, and make your play accordingly.

Less valuable are those tells that are voluntary (may be feigned), or those that could be either voluntary or involuntary -- you can't be sure; i.e., they are inconclusive. These types of tells also can be useful, but we need to take precautions so we will not be misled when observed.

Voluntary and Inconclusive Tells --

• Smiling; Head nodding up and down; Uttering positive words (like *"Oh boy"*);

• Looking at chips; Hand moving toward chips; Grabbing a stack of chips; Jiggling the chips;

• Appearing nervous; Fidgeting; Drumming fingers on table;

• A sad facial expression; Head moving from side to side; Uttering negative words (*"Oh shucks"* or *"Darn it"*); Shrugging shoulders;

• Counting the money in the pot;

• Checking the hole cards again and comparing them with the river card;

• Looking away from the table; Showing lack of interest.

These Voluntary and Inconclusive Tells can be utilized only if you have previously observed this player and correlated these tells with actual hands played. What did he have in his hand when this particular action was previously displayed? And, even in those cases, there may be considerable doubt.

In some cases, there are steps you can take to test for the validity or true meaning of these tells. *(We will discuss this below.)*

In Julius Fast's famous book, *Body Language*, he speaks of a "newly discovered kinesic signal" -- such as the unconscious widening of the pupil when the eye sees something pleasant. "On a useful plane," he wrote, "this can be of help in a poker game if the player is in the 'know.' When his opponent's pupils widen, he can be sure that his opponent is holding a good hand."* This is an example of an Involuntary Tell.

(Another interesting, albeit unrelated to poker, observation by Fast was that "a normal man's eye becomes twice as large when he sees a picture of a naked woman.")

Of course, players can be deceptive. For example, a player looks at his last card, and appears saddened; he shakes his head from side to side; he closes his eyes; he mutters some words under his breath; he pushes away from the table. These are tells that <u>seem</u> to inform you that he has not made the hand and will fold. But be careful.

Sometimes a devious poker player will feign such an action to fool you. If you know your opponents well enough by carefully observing their play and actions during other hands, you may be able to properly evaluate such tells.

A PokerPigeon is less likely to be deceptive; his tells are more likely to be valid. *(That's another good reason for playing at a table with lots of PokerPigeons.)*

---

* *Body Language* by Julius Fast; Pocket Books, Division of Simon & Schuster, New York, NY; 1970.

Sometimes there are ways to test the meaning of some Voluntary/Inconclusive Tells. Here is an example: If he appears nervous and is drumming his fingers on the table, make sure he is looking at you; and then deliberately and slowly move your betting hand (usually the right hand) to your stack of chips. Watch carefully to see if the nervous action stops as you take a batch of chips into your hand. If so, then he is most likely bluffing. If the drumming continues, he probably is not bluffing, and has in fact made a good hand.

If an opponent looks away from the table or up at the ceiling, implying disinterest, and <u>then</u> bets, you can be certain that he has a good hand. The same is the case if he shows a sad facial expression or utters some negative words, and then bets. *(If the hand was not good, why would he have bet?)*

Unconventional Tells

Once you have determined that a particular opponent is a PokerShark or a tight player, whenever he calls the opening bet you can be relatively certain that he holds a strong opening hand. While we may not regard this as a conventional tell, nevertheless it provides extremely valuable information. And there are other unconventional tells similar to this that are useful, but only if you have properly assessed your opponents.

For example, some players will always raise with a high pair on third street. Some players will only call when drawing to a straight or flush. Some will raise on fourth street with two pair (to force opponents to fold) but never with trips. In a spread-limit game, many players with very strong hands will make a small-to-modest bet on fourth street, and gradually increase the amount bet in each subsequent round. (They are trying to build up the pot by not forcing opponents out on early rounds.) If a tight player with a low-to-medium card showing as his upcard, raises on third street, chances are he has a high pair in the hole.

To use these unconventional tells, you need to know how those opponents play their cards. Generally, it is the better players who will bet in this manner. If you can do this, you are "reading" your opponents: Based on their upcards and betting pattern, you can figure out what hand each is holding. However, very loose and overly aggressive players are almost impossible to "read" in this way.

More Tells

Writing in the *Card Player* magazine,* Mike Caro (a well-known poker expert who has written books and lectured on poker) offers some interesting tells:

When you see a man "waving his money in the air and calling for chips" (whether he has just come to the table or has run out of chips at the table and needs a rebuy), that person is likely to play a loose game. (You should call his bets/raises more often because a loose player is more likely

---

* *Card Player*; Vol. 9, No. 13; June 28, 1996.

to try to bluff. And, conversely, you should attempt to bluff him less often because a loose player is more likely to call your bet when you attempt to bluff.)

On the other hand, when a player is carefully and cautiously going through his wallet (or her purse) to take out money to purchase chips, "that is a reflection of the player's true nature," according to Caro. And you should assume that he plays that way also: timidly. This is a tight player. That means you should drop out more often when he bets because a tight player is not likely to be bluffing; and you should bluff him more often because a tight player is more likely to fold with a marginal hand:

	When He Bets	When You Bluff
Loose Player --	May be bluffing	Likely to call
Tight Player --	Not likely to bluff	More likely to fold

Caro also recommends that you should call any bettor who covers his mouth as he makes the bet -- in the absence of indications to the contrary. Presumably this player is unconsciously "telling" you that he really doesn't have the hand he is representing, i.e., that he is bluffing.

In the same issue of *Card Player* magazine, another poker expert, Roy West, offers a valuable piece of advice relative to an interesting tell: While the final (seventh street) card is being dealt face down, West suggests that you "should look at your opponent rather than at the cards being dealt, like most players do." Observe your opponent as he looks at his river card. "If he looks at his last card

201

only a very short time, folds his cards together and glances at his chips, he made the hand and is ready to call all bets."

West observes that "many times, after having missed his hand, a player will allow a slight look of disgust to briefly cross his face, his shoulders might sag a bit, or he could become visibly disinterested in the hand. He might even show his cards to the friendly player next to him, in which case, he did not make the hand."

On the other hand, West suggests, "if he looks at his hole cards, then at his upcards, then at his hole cards, as do many recreational players *(many are PokerPigeons)*, he most likely is trying to figure out if he made a straight. It doesn't take much looking, even for a novice, to see if he made a flush or a full house."

Watch your opponent as the cards are being dealt. "If you are watching the seventh card being dealt around the table, or are looking at your seventh card, you'll miss all this," according to Roy West.

If you think about it -- and carefully observe your opponents during the game, you probably can identify many other possible tells. Indeed, these can be very valuable to you during the play of that hand and subsequent hands as well.

* * *

"Tells" in Life Situations

Just as other strategies from the game of poker can be applied to life, so too tells can be helpful in life situations as well. Expert sales people have learned to look at the customer's facial expressions and eyes -- using tells -- to close that sale; many top negotiators often rely on the opposition's mannerisms for clues on how best to direct the discussion to their own advantage so as to achieve the desired result. As noted in the Foreword, Lee Iacocca (who is credited with saving Chrysler Corp.) admitted to the use of his poker game learnings during "tough union negotiations." The use of tells can be a very effective tool in helping to realize one's goals in order to attain success, whatever the situation or circumstances.

In fact, you may be using tells in your daily life without realizing it. You watch her eyes while she speaks to you; somehow you can sense a message that goes beyond the spoken words.

Just as unintentional motions or facial expressions can provide valuable information in a poker game, so too in life we can gain valuable information in our dealings with other people. Whether you call it "body language" or the science of kinesics as suggested by some experts in the field, it is a fact that people will often "tell" you more by their motions or expressions than do their actual words.

For example, in his book, *Body Language*, Julius Fast explains how one young man was so successful in seducing young ladies -- while his friends watched in amazement. The young Romeo had learned how to send unspoken messages with his body motions, stance, and facial expressions (especially his eyes); and he received messages from his "quarry" in the same way. He had become expert in the art of body language -- "tells."

Famed comedian Groucho Marx perfected the movement of his eyebrows — called the "eyebrow flash" — to express non-verbal messages that his audiences easily understood. Actually, raised eyebrows are used not only to flirt with a pretty girl as did Groucho, but also may serve to express agreement, show surprise or fear, or sometimes disapproval or disbelief. The real message to be conveyed depends on the circumstances at that time.

A study at the University of Santa Cruz, California, noted that the eyes, brows and forehead "are more authentic than the lower face, which we use to perform polite smiling and other things."* Psychologist Dana Archer points out: "If we are trying to mask our feelings, we do it with our lower face. The upper face is under less control." The point, of course, is that tells are more often received from the eyes, brows and forehead. Therefore, if you are observing an opponent for a tell, it would be wise to concentrate on his upper face; these tells are less likely to be deceptive.

> *Of course, other aspects of the game of poker can be applied to life situations. But that would be the subject of another book.* — George Epstein

* * *

If you have made mistakes. . .
there is always another chance for you. . . .
You may have a fresh start any moment you choose,
for this thing we call "failure" is not the falling down,
but the staying down.
-- Mary Pickford

---

* *"The Strangest Species"* by Kathleen Kelleher;
Los Angeles Times newspaper; August 19, 1996.

• <u>STRATEGY ON CARD-TRACKING</u>

The better you are at keeping track of the cards played, the greater is your advantage over the other players -- and the more likely you are to win more money. Most seven-card stud players use only the cards still exposed on the board to make their decisions. PokerSharks try to remember those that have been folded also, because they provide a wealth of additional information. Watch the cards exposed and then folded during the deal; try to remember them -- especially the high cards and those that relate to your hand and to those of the players who stay in the pot. Concentrate on the cards being folded; that's much easier then trying to remember all the upcards. (After all, the upcards not folded are still in full view.)

If you are new to card-tracking, it may be difficult at first; but, with practice, you can hone your skills. *(It's also healthy for your mind by exercising your memory.)*

Why is card-tracking so valuable? If you know, for example, that three aces have been exposed with only one in an active opponent's hand, then you know that he could have only two aces at most -- obviously not three aces. He is most likely to be holding two pair, aces-up, or just the pair of aces. If you are holding three kings, your chances of winning are much greater than your opponent's. You can bet and play accordingly.

Suppose your opponent shows 4♣ 5♦ 7♠ 8♣ on the board. He would need a six in the hole to have a straight. During the course of the hand, you observed two sixes folded by other players, and you have a third six in the hole. You are, of course, in a more knowledgeable position than if none of the sixes had shown. There is only one possible six remaining, out of, perhaps, thirty unseen cards; only 1 chance in 30 that he has it! But you must remember that information if it is to be of value to you.

How can you remember all the cards that have been folded?

That's a tough question. Certainly, it's hard to remember them all, but whatever you can remember will help.

Here's one way: Bear in mind that you need to keep track only of the cards discarded as each player folds his hand. Observe the cards as they are dealt out but <u>only</u> try to memorize the discarded cards. Repeat under your breath the cards that were folded in some sort of order. For example, start with the highest cards and count up from 8 to ace; and then start with the lowest cards and count up from 2 to 7 -- or vice versa.

Suppose, on third street, you observe a ten folded by one player; a queen by another; a four by another; and a five by still another. Under your breath, silently repeat:

ten, queen; four, five.

And make a mental picture: 10 - Q; 4 - 5. Sometimes it helps to put the numbers in combinations, such as 45 instead of 4 - 5.

On the next round, suppose you observe another player fold a ten and a four. Then, under your breath, silently say:

double ten - queen; double four - five.

And mentally, picture: double 10 - Q; double 4 - 5.

Continue in this way as the hand progresses, observing and remembering all of the cards that have been folded. *(In fact, you can mumble under your breath if it helps you to remember the cards folded.)* Try to picture them in your mind; that can be a big help. Relate them to your hand if appropriate. If you have a 4 and a queen, that makes it easier to remember that two 4s and one queen have been folded.

If a player happens to reveal his hole cards as he folds, add those to your list to remember.

Sometimes an opponent will turn his cards over so quickly that it is hard to observe them, or perhaps even out of turn. To deal with such situations -- which are not uncommon -- you should look ahead several seats beyond the player whose turn it is to bet. Also, when it is your turn to bet, you can hesitate long enough to examine the upcards of the players to your left who have yet to bet.

Make a special effort to remember the value of those cards that have been folded previously. If on the next round, fifth street in this case, you observe a player fold with a deuce, queen, and four, pay special attention to the fact that three fours and two queens have been folded.

It's more difficult to remember the suits that have been folded, yet that is also valuable information. If an opponent shows four clubs on the board, but you know that six clubs have been folded and there are two additional clubs exposed in the other players' hands -- for a total of eight clubs, then you know that it is very unlikely that the opponent has the club flush, and you can bet accordingly. On the opening deal, try to observe if three or more of any suit is exposed. Make a mental note of that information and try to add to it as the hand progresses. Likewise, if you see several of another suit dealt out, make a mental note. Even if you only recall that a large number of a particular suit were exposed, without remembering the number, that information can be useful.

A device to aid this effort is to use your chips: Place a chip to the left of your stack if you observe three clubs (C) on the board. Place a chip on the table just above that if it is three diamonds (D); to the right of your stack if it is three spades (S); and just above that if it is three hearts (H). Then, as additional cards of that suit are folded, add one chip for each.:

Stack of Chips

By the time you reach seventh street, if you have six chips in, say, the spades group, that means that eight spades have been folded (the original chip for three spades plus five additional ones).

That can be extremely valuable information if an opponent has four spades in his upcards. With eight spades folded, he would have to have the case spade to hold a flush. And, if that card happens to be one of your hole cards, you know he could not possibly have a spade flush!

What If I Miss Some?

It's OK if you miss or forget a few of the folded upcards; no one is perfect. The more you remember, the better, because it will help you make the right decisions. Knowing whatever cards you can recall that were folded, plus the cards showing on the table, and your own cards, of course, gives you valuable information that can make a BIG difference in how you play or bet a hand. *(In fact, that is one reason why I prefer playing seven-card stud over Texas hold'em and other poker games.)*

In playing seven-card stud, try to remember the cards that have been folded. The information can be extremely valuable in deciding how best to play your hand and betting.

---

* * *

The difference between winning and losing may be the $ you didn't bet with a losing hand.

• <u>STRATEGY FOR BETTING ON THE RIVER</u>

Without question, a strategy for betting on the last card is extremely important. At this point, you probably have made a significant investment in the hand, and the pot may contain quite a bit of money (which you would like to add to your stack).

This strategy is so important, in fact, that it should be read carefully -- even though we are repeating some of the discussion presented earlier.

The best way to address this strategy is through example. Let's suppose you hold a fairly decent hand after the last downcard has been dealt on the river -- say, two pair, queens-up. Your hand is high on the table. Should you come out betting? If you can "stand a raise" (i.e., your hand is good enough so that you would call a raise), then it is proper to make the maximum bet on the last round of betting. If not, then you should check -- and, if you have a chance of winning, call the bet if someone else makes it.

No matter how strong an opponent's hand appears, if there is a sizable pot (i.e., the pot odds are high) and you are not beaten on the table, then you must call the bet. *(We have said this before!)* He may be bluffing! It happens quite often. On sixth street an opponent bet on an "apparent" flush; at least that is what he seemed to be representing. For the sake of this example, let's say you hold two pair. Now the seventh -- and last -- card is dealt. And, unfortunately, it does not improve your hand. Still, your hand is high on the board; you check. Your opponent quickly bets the maximum. You take another look at your hole cards; you have missed the full house. You feel inclined to fold your cards because you didn't make the hand for which you were looking. . . Don't succumb to this natural inclination. Don't drop out. Don't give up. Call that last bet -- unless the pot odds are very poor. It is almost certain that the pot odds are high enough to warrant a call. It is worth the relatively small investment in case your opponent does not have the hand he is representing. Lo and behold, in such a situation, frequently you end up winning the pot with your two pair!

I have seen many players make the mistake of folding with cards that might have taken the pot. This strategy should be taken very seriously. Imagine how you would feel when your opponent takes a pot with a hand lower than yours, as he proudly shows off his hand to all of the players at the table -- while he scoops in his reward that could have been yours.

Seventh street also provides a good opportunity for selective aggressive betting. If no great strength has been shown during the hand, consider making the bet on the river -- even if you expect that an opponent has a better hand. Further, if you hold a hand with which you would call a bet by an opponent, and no one has bet before you, by all means make the bet. Act like you have a great hand and bet it boldly and confidently. Your opponent(s) may believe you and fold; besides, you may actually have the best hand. You may get called, but even if you don't have the winning hand sometimes, those times you do will more than make up for the times you are called and lose. In fact, many PokerPigeons will fold the moment you bet, even if they have your hand beaten, because they will "be sure" you have made a good hand.

Summary of Strategy for Betting on the River

• **If you are high on the board, make the bet if you can stand a raise.**

• **If an opponent bets, call so long as your hand is not beaten on the board.**

• **If there is no great strength among the other players, bet aggressively.**

• **If no one has bet before you and you hold a hand with which you would call a bet, then you should make the bet first; and bet aggressively.**

---

* * *

I've learned...
Never to humiliate another person.
Always give him/her an honorable way
to back down or out of something
and still save face. -- Anonymous

• __RAISING WITH THE BEST HAND ON THE RIVER__

This strategy is a special case of Betting on the River. In this case, you have the best hand and want to maximize your winnings by getting as much $ into the pot as possible. Should you raise? Should you check-raise?

Here's the situation: You have made an almost certain winning hand on the last card, and two or more opponents showing strong hands on the board are still in the hand. Should you raise when the betting gets around to you? Remember, you expect to win the pot. At this point you are trying to increase the size of the pot. For the sake of discussion, let's say you hold aces-full-of-tens with two of the aces in the hole, and you show just the pair of tens on the board.

In a spread-limit game, if you are high on the table and therefore the first to declare, and if it is a tight game, it would be wise to bet less than the maximum -- say $3.00 in a $1-$5 spread-limit game. With a modest bet, you are more likely to get at least one caller. You might even get a raise from an opponent who has made his hand on the last card; and, in that case, you could reraise. On the other hand, if the remaining opponents are loose players, you should bet the maximum ($5.00 in this example).

Hopefully you were correct in your assessment that you held the best hand. Remember, with three downcards there is always the possibility of a four-of-a-kind or even a straight flush. But the probabilities highly favor you in such a maneuver -- especially if you have observed many of your opponents' matching card among the other players' upcards.

If you are playing in a structured-limit stakes game, there are just two choices: You can either check or bet the specified amount. For example, in a $3-$6 structured-limit game, your bet would be $6.00. It is prudent in such cases to make the bet and hope one or more of the other players will call you. Usually at least one will call unless your up-cards are extremely strong. An opponent with a strong hand may even raise, in which case you could reraise.

How About a Check-Raise?

This is a maneuver where you check in the hope that an opponent will bet; and then you raise in order to earn an extra bet. Check-raise is allowed in most poker rooms. *(Sometimes it is frowned upon in home games.)* It can be useful when you hold a monster hand or, better yet, the nuts so you know that you cannot lose.

Check-raise is a reasonable approach if there are several players in the hand on the river, but less desirable if you are playing heads up. Unless one of your opponents has been raising all along (i.e., he is aggressive) and shows a strong hand, it is likely that the final bet will be checked all around should you elect to try for a check-raise. Therefore you should attempt the check-raise only if you are playing against a loose-aggressive player who has been betting and raising during the hand, and you believe that your check would get others to call his bet before you raised. In that case, the loose-aggressive player should be seated near to your left. If he is seated near to your right, the check-raise maneuver would not be advisable; make your bet.

A check-raise can also be detrimental, because it alerts an opponent to the fact that you may hold a hand even stronger than his. Had you bet and he raised, then your reraise would be less likely to set off alarm warnings, thereby encouraging further raises -- and greater winnings for you! (We will illustrate this in an example in the Comments at the end of this strategy discussion.)

Holding the best hand on the river, if you are the second to bet during the final round and there are two or more players behind you yet to bet, it would be wise to simply call. A raise would likely drive out the remaining players. Simply calling the bet could encourage one or more of the other players to call or possibly even raise the pot. Should one of the opponents raise, examine his hand carefully; consider (if you can) all of the upcards that have fallen and how the remaining "live" cards might affect the raiser's hand. If you are still convinced that you have the best hand, then go ahead and reraise when the betting comes around to you. If there is a chance the raiser could beat you (perhaps with a higher full house, four-of-a-kind, or even a straight flush), you should call only. *(Under no circumstances should you drop out at this point; you have too much money invested in the pot; the pot odds are bound to be favorable; and the raiser may be bluffing.)*

On the other hand, if the high hand on the table has bet and at least one other player before you has called, a raise would be appropriate -- regardless of the number of players to your left who have yet to bet. Chances are that at least one opponent will call your raise. But here some judgment is warranted: If you expect one of the players yet to bet will make the raise, then simply calling would be prudent -- with the intention of reraising when the betting reached you again.

If, under the same circumstances, you are one of the last to bet, then it is appropriate for you to make your raise. If anyone calls you, fine. If not, the pot is as large as you could hope to make it. However, if you are reraised, you should assess that player's hand before raising again. Certainly you will want to call his raise, but do not reraise if there is a chance that your hand may be second best.

Comments

There will be many occasions when several players are holding strong hands. I have been in hands where three players (including myself) held full houses. And then there was the hand where three players all made flushes. My king-high was second to an ace-high flush. The ace was hidden in the hole! It can be quite expensive when you are second- or third-best. *(I know!)*

On another occasion, I made four nines on the river! I was high on board with two nines showing and bet into the only remaining active player who showed a pair of sixes. He raised. The best hand he could have was four sixes. I had him beaten with my four nines; so I reraised. (I did it quickly to keep the momentum going and to discourage his "taking a breath to think.")

We raised each other again and again until he ran out of chips. (In most poker casinos, the "House Rules" do not allow you to "go into your pocket" for more money once the cards are dealt. Only the chips in front of you "play;" i.e., can be used in the betting -- although some poker rooms do allow players to use any cash on the table along with the chips, most often in high-stakes games.) I loved those four nines and the great pot!

This hand is an example where a check-raise would have been detrimental to my best interests. Had I checked my four nines, assuming he had a very strong hand (of which I could not be sure), and then raised his bet, that immediately would make him suspicious of my motive. If he held only sixes-full rather than four sixes, my check-raise would have alerted him to the possibility that I had nines-full or better. Then he would have simply called my raise; and I would not have "earned" all that additional $ from the wild spree of raises.

* * *

It's better to be an optimist. Here's why. . .
No pessimist ever discovered the secrets of the stars.
or sailed to an uncharted land,
or opened a new heaven to the human spirit.

-- Helen Keller

• DRINKING WHILE PLAYING POKER; YOUR MENTAL AND PHYSICAL STATE

One of the four Basic Rules warns against drinking alcoholic beverages while playing poker. We can regard this rule as a strategy too. A strategy is a plan for reaching a goal or gaining an advantage under a given set of conditions. If you keep your mind alert while your opponents are enjoying alcoholic beverages, then it goes without saying that you are at a decided advantage. You are better able to track the cards played, to assess your opponents' hands and actions, and to make wiser decisions.

Of course, the same applies to taking drugs, even if they are medications prescribed by your doctor. If the container warns you to avoid driving or operating equipment after taking the drug, you should heed and apply that advice -- and avoid playing poker while under its influence. To reiterate Basic Poker Rule #4, it would be preferable to take the medication after leaving the poker game.

Likewise, a PokerShark is wise enough not to play when he is tired, angry, ill, or irritable. You need your complete faculties available so you can play your best game. Give yourself every possible advantage within your control. Try to be in your best form whenever you sit at the poker table. Concentrate on the game. . .

* * *

It's great fun to be a winner. -- Irene Epstein

218

CHAPTER FIVE --
RULES AND STRATEGIES
FOR TEXAS HOLD'EM:

by Dr. Daniel E. Abrams

Texas hold'em (often referred to simply as hold'em) has become the most popular poker game in America. At a California casino on any given afternoon, one might find five hold'em games, three seven-card stud games, one seven-card high-low split game, and one hold'em/Omaha high-low mixed game in the high-end section.

Why has hold'em become so popular? Probably because it is a faster-paced game than stud; the action tends to be faster, and the pots are proportionately larger. Unlike stud, the ability to memorize the cards on the board is not a factor. This is a plus for many poker players who find trying to remember the cards a tiresome and onerous task. On the other hand, because betting begins after two downcards are dealt to each player -- no upcards, the initial investment is based solely on these two downcards. You have no other information as would be provided if there were any upcards (as in seven-card stud). As a consequence, the initial betting can be quite lively, with lots of raising and reraising, and possibly a good deal of bluffing.

219

Like other games of poker, there are essentially three variations of hold'em based on the limits:

• Limit Hold'em -- In this game, the betting stakes may range from a low of $1-$2 to a high of $5,000-$10,000 *(or more)*.

• Pot-Limit Hold'em -- The betting structure here is different from the above in that the maximum bet is determined by the amount of $ already in the pot. Any player may bet any amount up to this limit at any time.

• No-Limit Hold'em -- There is no limit as to how much any player may bet at any time. The only limit is the amount of money the player has on the table.

Structure of the Game

In Texas hold'em poker, there are either nine or ten players at a full table, plus a dealer who typically works for the house. When a new game starts, each player selects a seat. You may make a special request for a seat when you sign up to play. The dealer shuffles the cards and spreads them face down on the table. Each player selects one card to determine who will begin with the "button" (sometimes called the "dealer"). The player who selects the highest card will have the button placed in front of him on the table.

The two players seated immediately to the left of the button must post (or ante) a "small" and a "big" blind, respectively. The amounts of these blinds are determined by the game limit, with the big blind equal to the lowest bet allowed, and the small blind just one-half that amount. For example, in a $2-$4 limit game, the small blind would be $1.00, and the big blind would be $2.00. Similarly, in

220

a $20-$40 game, the small blind would be $10.00, and the big blind would be $20.00. These are "forced" bets or antes since the player must put up this money before the cards are dealt -- hence the term "blinds." The cards are then dealt out beginning with the player with the small blind (seated immediately to the left of the button), then the player with the big blind, and then the remaining players, with the button ("dealer") receiving his cards last. Each player receives two cards, face down.

The first player to declare -- by folding, calling, or raising the big blind bet -- is the player to the left of the big blind. After the betting has moved around the table past the "button," the player with the small blind then has the option to add an amount to his forced bet -- matching the previous bet (or raises) in order to stay in the game; or he can raise or fold. The big blind then has the option to call, or initiate a raise.

At the end of each hand, the button is moved clockwise to the next player, along with the required blinds.

If you sit down at a game already in progress, you may begin to play by two different means. First, you can wait until you are the big blind and, at that point, put up the necessary amount. That means you may sit out a number of hands while waiting. Alternatively, most casinos allow you to "post," i.e., put up the amount of $ in the big blind. You will then be dealt a hand. The second way is generally preferred since you only have to pay one "blind" instead of two, until after the button comes around to you again.

As with stud games, you are not allowed to remove your cards from the table. *(Also, of course, you should be careful that you do not allow any of the other players to see your cards).*

If you leave the table and miss your turn at being the "blind," the dealer will put a "missed blind" marker on the table in front of your chips. When you return to the table, you will be required to post the blind in order to re-enter the game immediately, or you may wait until it is your turn to put up the blind.

In hold'em, like stud games, there is usually a limit of three raises when three or more players are in the hand. There is no limit on the number of raises when there are only two players remaining in the hand. After the initial round of betting (called "pre-flop" betting), the dealer will "burn" a card *(just as in seven-card stud)*. Then he will deal off the next three cards from the deck and place them face up in the center of the table. This is called the "flop." These are "community cards" each player may use as part of his hand. After the flop is made, the betting is clockwise, beginning with the player to the seat just to the left of the button. The dealer then burns the top card in the deck, and turns over another community card in the center of the table next to the "flop" cards. This card is often referred to as the "turn card." The betting then continues, as before. Finally, the dealer burns a card, and turns over the fifth and last community card -- known as the river card. The final betting round then occurs in the same order as before.

The object of the game is to make the highest possible five-card poker hand using any combination of the seven cards available to you (your two downcards and the five community cards). It is possible to "play the board" in which case only the five community cards are used and none of the downcards.

After the final round of betting, the dealer asks the players to reveal their cards. Remember to turn your cards up in front of you. You may, but need not, declare your hand. It is the job of the dealer to "read" each player's hand, "kill" the hands not revealed, announce the winner, and push the pot to the player with the winning hand. *If you have the best (winning) hand, do not reach for the pot; allow the dealer to push it to you.*

At high limits, players often verbally declare their hands, sometimes prior to exposing them. Make sure that you do not throw away your hand based on another player's verbal declaration. Wait until he turns over the hand and you can see what it is. Also, do not rely on the dealer's declaration of the hand. Look at it yourself and decide if you agree. *It doesn't happen often, but sometimes dealers make mistakes.* If you cannot see the hand, it is appropriate that you ask the dealer to bring it closer to you so that you can verify the declaration. *It is not allowed for any player to touch another player's hand, even after it has been revealed. (It is wrong to show your hand to another player at the table during the hand, even if that player is not involved in the hand.)*

If you lose, you may turn your hand over, or you may throw your cards into the muck. *(As noted previously in discussing the game of seven-card stud, the "muck" is the pile of killed cards the dealer collects during the hand, and is kept separate from the burn cards.)* However, as with other forms of poker, any player may request to see any called hand. If a player asks to see your called hand, you must allow him to do so. If you place your cards face down, the dealer will touch them to the muck to "kill" your hand and then turn them face up for all to see.

Special House Regulations for Texas Hold'em

What happens at the end of a hand when neither player wants to expose his hand first? The general rule is that the player who made the last bet that was called must expose his hand first. To clarify, let's assume that on the river, the player in seat No. 3 checks; the player in seat No. 6 bets; and seat No. 3 calls. Seat No. 6 must reveal his cards first. However, if seat No 3 were to raise and seat No. 6 then called, then seat No. 3 would be required to reveal his cards first. If no one bets on the river, then the player in the earliest seat must turn over his hand first.

Now, how about this one: The betting is over and both players turn their hands over. The dealer misreads the hands and (mistakenly) "kills" the best hand by putting it into the muck. What happens? If the player with the best hand sees this, he immediately should protest and state that his hand was better. The dealer will try to retrieve that player's cards from the muck. If he can, the dealer will turn them over again, and correctly award the pot to the best hand.

It is important to note that dealers, under such circumstances, should immediately call a floorperson to resolve the problem. If the dealer cannot retrieve the correct two cards, the floorperson usually will first ask the dealer what the two cards were. If the dealer doesn't know, the floorperson will probably ask the other players if they saw the two cards. If any of the other players can identify the cards, usually the floorperson will award the pot to the correct winning hand (which the dealer had mucked). If no one can identify the two cards, you have the option of asking the floorperson to "check the camera." Not all tables in all casinos are videotaped, but some are. The floorperson will review the tape, if available, and use this information to award the pot correctly. In this circumstance, the floorperson will ask the dealer to count the pot and set it aside so the exact amount can be awarded after the tape review is completed. However, if the player who incorrectly received the pot concedes that the other hand was better than his, the problem is solved and the player who received the pot incorrectly simply gives the amount to the player who really had the best hand. (On some occasions, the two players involved may agree to split the pot.)

It is the responsibility of each player to protect his hand at all times. Keep the cards near you, and either keep a hand on them or place a chip (or a good luck token) on top of them. *I personally never let loose of my cards during a hand.*

Should a dealer inadvertently scoop your cards into the muck, you are out of luck. You are then out of the hand and cannot receive your cards back. This is also true if it happens at the end of a hand. *How painful it is if the dealer scoops ("kills") your hand accidentally while you were still thinking of calling!*

"Chopping" or splitting the pot is another fairly frequent occurrence in hold'em. If a hand is called and two (or more) players have exactly the same hand, then the dealer will evenly divide the pot among all players with the same winning hand. Another form of chopping often occurs before the flop. Sometimes most of the players will fold, leaving only the small and big blinds with money in the pot. In this situation it is common for one to ask, "Do you want to chop?" meaning that he does not wish to play the hand heads up. If both players agree, then each simply takes back his blind bet; the dealer moves the button and deals another hand. Almost all casinos allow this form of chopping a pot. It is always your option to chop or not. Both players must agree to it, throw in their cards, and retrieve their blinds. In this case, the dealer does not get involved.

Sometimes, a player may ask to chop a hand after the flop. For example, let's say seat No. 10 raises, and only the big blind calls. The raiser then says, "Do you want to chop?" This is technically illegal and against regulations in many casinos. Another player may protest and ask for a floorperson to make the decision. You may even see a player ask to chop even later in the hand, even after the river card. Again, this usually is not allowed and any player may object.

Another interesting hold'em situation has to do with instances where no player can beat the cards on the board (the community cards face up on the table). Let's say, for example, that the board consists of a full house:

K-K-K-J-J

and none of the calling players can better this community hand with his downcards. In this situation, you may turn your hand face up, or you may declare, "I'll play the board." *Do not, however, throw your cards into the muck or you will lose the chance to divide the pot with the other players remaining in the hand.*

There are situations in hold'em where a misdeal may be declared. In these situations, the players must surrender their cards and the dealer will re-shuffle and re-deal the hand correctly. For example, the dealer may neglect to deal in a player who should have received a hand, or includes a player who should not have received a hand. Occasionally, a player ends up with the wrong number of cards (one card or three cards, instead of two). It is also a misdeal if it is discovered at any point during the hand that the deck is not correct; e.g., there are two tens of spades. If this happens, the hand will be ruled "no action," and all money in the pot will be returned to the appropriate players. A misdeal will be called if the first card dealt is turned face up by mistake.

There are some scenarios that you might expect to be misdeals, but are not. Some examples:

• If a card other than the first one dealt is turned face up by mistake, the dealer will "kill" only that card, but continue dealing in sequence. The last card dealt will be a face-down card to the player who originally received the face-up card.

227

• If a marked or damaged card is discovered during a hand, the hand will play and the deck will then be changed.

• If a card is dealt off the table, and falls onto the floor, landing face down, the player will be allowed to keep it. If it lands face up, the player may exchange it for another.

The Basic Poker Rules Applied to Hold'em

My co-author, George Epstein, has described the Four Basic Rules for winning at poker as applied to seven-card stud. (See Chapter 2.) These same rules apply to Texas hold'em with some modifications only for Rule #3.

Rule #3: Don't Lose! Play Only Those Hands You Have a Good Chance of Winning.

As in seven-card stud, the major difference between winning and losing in hold'em is the selection of hands to play before the flop. PokerPigeons stay in too many hands *(as in other poker games as well).* Certain hands should not be played from the start (pre-flop) with the possible exception of whether you are one of the "blinds" and, hence, have already paid the price. These combinations are listed in the Appendix.

MOST IMPORTANT ARE THE HANDS WORTHY OF THE INITIAL INVESTMENT.

The top four starting hands in hold'em are a pair of aces, kings, or queens, and A-K suited — in that order. These powerful hands should be played from any position. You should raise aggressively and hope that you have and keep the lead. *Some would argue that an A-K suited should not be played aggressively, but I do because of the value of the possible nut flush. I believe that you will do just fine overall playing this hand aggressively and strongly.*

Now, if you were a "super rock" and decided you would only play these top four hands and no others, in the long run you might be a winning player at any level — unless the blinds "ate up" all your chips while you waited.. So it helps to rate the possible starting hands:

Starting Hand Values

Value	Downcards	Suited?	Unsuited?
Best:	A-A, K-K, Q-Q	N/A	N/A
	A-K	Yes	No
Medium:	J-J, 10-10, 9-9	N/A	N/A
	A-Q, A-J, A-10,	Yes	Yes
	K-Q, K-J, K-10	Yes	Yes
Borderline:	A-9 through A-6	Yes	Yes
	K-9 through K-6	Yes	No
	Q-J, Q-10, J-10	Yes	Yes
	10-9, 10-8, 9-8	Yes	Yes
	8-7, 7-6, 6-5, 5-4	Yes	No
	8-8, 7-7, 6-6, 5-5	N/A	N/A

This table shows groupings of starting hands based on value. (The first ones listed are more valuable and hence preferred over the others in the grouping — in the order shown.) By way of explanation, A-K suited is ranked among the "Best;" however, A-K unsuited would drop to the next lower rank and is regarded as "Medium."

The four best hands — A-A, K-K, Q-Q, or A-K suited — should be played in any position. No matter where you are seated at the table, stay in the hand to see the flop. On the other hand, the decision to play medium hands depends on position and the number of bets it will cost. Borderline hands should <u>only</u> be played when you have good position (one of the last to bet) and several players stay in to help build the pot if you make your hand.

In applying this table, it is advisable <u>not</u> to play any hand lower in value than the ones listed <u>unless</u> you are the big blind and no one has raised; i.e., it doesn't cost you to stay in to see the turn card. (See also the Appendix.) However, there are exceptions depending on how your opponents play (loose or tight), your table position, the betting, and the number of players in the pot when the betting reaches you. For example, an ace-rag* <u>suited</u> has value as a starting hand in a loose game and especially if there has not been more than one raise. This is because of the possibility of the nut flush hand (ace-high flush), and not for the value of the ace should you pair it up.

When deciding which hand to play before the flop, err in the direction of being too tight (or over-conservative), and you won't go wrong.

* * *

---

* A "rag" is a card that usually does not help the hand, and is not likely to be of value. But in this case, with an ace of the same suit, it could help to make an ace-high flush.

Strategies for Texas Hold'em

Describing the best strategies for Texas hold'em is a daunting task because it is so influenced by your assessment of the opponents and table position. For example, in a very tight game with good players *(lots of PokerSharks)*, if you are in seat No. 6 and two players have raised, you can be fairly certain your pair of tens is beaten. However, in a very loose game with average or poor *players (lots of PokerPigeons)*, a double raise in front of you is much less intimidating and your pair of tens may well be top hand.

Your table position -- relative to the betting sequence -- is extremely important in hold'em. Hands in early positions have less value than hands in late positions. The reason is that players in the later positions have the great benefit of seeing what all the players do in front of them, before making a decision. *That is why good players try to use position to control the betting and the game.*

Strategies for Pre-Flop Betting

Special attention should be given to the pre-flop opening round of betting.

• When all but one player has folded, and you are the small or big blind, never chop these hands if it provides an opportunity to play heads-up against someone who you believe is not as good a player as you.

Once, in a $40-$80 hold'em game, someone asked me to chop. I said no. The other player persisted: "Why not?" I couldn't resist saying, "I only chop if Johnny Chan is on one side and Phil Hellmuth is on the other."

• If you are the small blind and no one has called -- so that only you and the big blind remain in the pot -- and your hand has a jack or better, you should raise. If not, fold your hand.

• If only one player remains in the hand on the opening round, and you are the big blind, jack or better is worth a raise and ace-rag is worth two raises. Most hold'em players don't realize that an ace with any other card is favored when played heads-up against any other two unpaired cards, including K-Q suited.

> Here is an amusing anecdote. *(It could be true.)* It concerns the two tightest players in the long history of poker: "Mr. Tightest I" and "Mr. Tightest II" were in a limit hold'em championship tournament event. They reached the final table and after several hours, it became heads-up between the two of them. Each vowed not to lose -- no matter what. Hours went by and neither played a hand. Finally, after 24 hours with the blinds now at $100,000 - $200,000, Mr. Tightest I raised. Mr. Tightest II looked at his hand and found pocket aces. So, he raised back. Mr. Tightest I reraised. The reraising continued until they were both all in. Yes, you guessed it: They both had pocket aces. At this point, they decided to quit and split the prize pool.

• Use the implied odds to your advantage. It is important to understand the concepts of "pot odds" and "implied pot odds." Let's say, for example, that you have two fives in seat position No. 6 in a lively $1-$4-$8-$8 hold'em game and no one raises to you. You call the $1.00 big blind, and so do five others. Now, the odds of flopping a set (three fives) are 8-to-1 against you. Since there is $6.00 in the pot, you are getting 6-to-1 pot odds -- not bad because the actual card odds are fairly close to the pot odds. More important are the implied pot odds -- the $ you could presume to win if you flop your set (three fives). In a loose game with this betting structure, the implied pot odds could easily be much more favorable than 8-to-1 against you; hence it is worth the $1.00 investment to see the flop. By contrast, suppose you have a pair of fives in position No. 6, someone raises to $4.00, and everyone folds. Then it is not worth risking $4.00 (assuming you believe the raiser can beat your pair of fives). With only the raiser still in the hand, the implied pot odds are just too poor.

• To be a successful hold'em player, resolve to never play hands not shown in our table of starting hands -- with the few exceptions noted above. It may be tempting, but do not stay in with K-rag suited; Q-rag suited; any other two cards unsuited below J-10; and finally, avoid playing A-rag unsuited. This latter hand separates the average player from the poor player. (The poor player believes that A-rag unsuited is a good hand.) The reason A-rag unsuited is a poor starting hand is that when an ace flops, frequently another player will also have an ace, but he will have a higher kicker -- and so your hand will be second-best.

Post-Flop Strategy

The most basic concept for winning at hold'em (and other forms of poker) is that you want to start with the best hand, bet aggressively, and end up with the best hand.

Thus, if you start with the best hand pre-flop, then you do not need help on the flop; you simply need your opponents to not catch up. Thus, if you start with a pair of kings, and the flop is Q-10-7, offsuit, you can reasonably assume you still have the best hand. So you bet, and someone raises. You hope/assume your opponent has a queen or a ten; so you raise back. He calls. The turn is a 3; you bet and again are called. The river is a 4, you bet and again he calls. You turn your kings over; your opponent turns over K-Q. You win the pot! (*I promise you that sometime this will happen.*)

Now, on the other hand, you start with kings and the flop comes A-10-7 unsuited. There are four players against you. Do you bet -- or do you check, assuming one of the four has an ace? This decision depends on your assessment of the opponents; but since there is an excellent chance that someone has an ace, the safe bet is no bet. As a general rule, when you do not have top pair after the flop, you are behind and must surrender your hand. It takes a very good and disciplined player -- a PokerShark -- to fold these big kings when an ace flops and a good player bets ahead of you; but you must do this if you are to succeed. Lay it down and wait until the next hand. Sure, once in a while this player in front of you will turn over Q-10 (in the above scenario) and you will kick yourself for folding the best hand, but you will, over the long run, save money.

The second strategy in post-flop play is that if you have a very strong hand, one that beats top pair; e.g., two pair or a set (three-of-a-kind), you should wait until the turn to raise. For example, suppose that you have Q-10 suited, and the flop comes Q-10-7 unsuited. The leader bets with his pocket kings. What do you do if there is no one behind you? You only call. Then, you raise on the turn card as long as it is neither an ace nor a king. Generally, you want to play a set the same way. Wait until the turn to raise, since the turn bet is double the amount.

But there are always exceptions. You may want to raise right after the flop when you make a set, particularly if it is <u>not</u> top set (i.e., the highest possible three-of-a-kind), and especially if there are two suited cards in the flop, and more than two opponents in the hand. This is because you want to make the players on flush draws pay the maximum for the right to see the turn card; and also you would be improving your chances of winning the pot if an opponent decides to fold as a result of your raise.

What About Drawing Hands?

Regarding drawing hands, if you have followed our previous advice, you are working only on the nut flush (highest flush possible), or the nut straight -- ace-high in each case. If you do not flop two (out of the three) cards with the suit you need (in a flush draw); or, to give you four cards in sequence for the straight for which you are hoping; or you do not have top pair, dump the hand. Fold.

For example, if you start with A-5 of hearts and the flop comes 10-6-J, two hearts, you have the nut flush draw and should call any number of raises. But what if the flop comes A-10-7 with only one heart, and a good player bets. In that case, you must put him on a "big ace" (an ace with a big kicker) and lay your hand down. This is another situation that separates the good players from the bad. Remember, the value of hands like A-5 suited is not the ace, but the possibility of obtaining the nut flush.

What About Slow-Playing?

Generally, slow-playing hands in Texas hold'em is not recommended, but there is one exception. When you have the nuts after the flop, you should check. For example, you have a pair of kings and the flop comes K-K-A. Don't bet; you should check. Slow-play your hand. If no one bets, you should probably check on the turn as well, especially if the game is tight. You are hoping that one or more of your opponents will improve his hand; and you don't want to lose opponents should they fold as a result of a bet. Should an opponent bet, you might consider making a raise.

However, if you are a beginning player, don't worry about slow-playing hands. Instead, develop the philosophy that you want to start with the lead, bet aggressively, hold the lead, and win the pot.

Bluffing

The strategy for buffing in Texas hold'em is very similar to that for seven-card stud. But, because it is so important, we will discuss it again here.

Let's define a bluff as betting your hand (or raising) when you are relatively sure that someone else has a better hand, and you will surely lose the pot if you do not bet. The decision to bluff must be based on your evaluation of your opponents and the particular situation. If you are in a game where every hand is called to the river, then there is little point to a bluff. But, if you are in a game where the pot is not often called on the river, you have the opportunity to win without the best hand. *If I am in the latter game, I will literally keep betting until no one calls. After all, if your adversaries are willing to give you free money, why not accept it?* Now, if you are employing this aggressive, keep-betting strategy, and finally do get called on the end, turn your cards over and let everyone see. As noted previously, when you do get caught in a bluff, this "advertising" can be useful the next time you have a big hand. More likely than not, an opponent will call your bet or raise, remembering the time you bluffed, and thinking you might be bluffing again.

Bluffing is part of a good player's arsenal. If you never bluff, then pretty soon good players will note this fact and never call when you bet unless they have a strong hand. *Why should they?*

A final consideration is the relationship between bluffing and position. It is much easier to bluff and win when you are the last to act. In this situation, let's say that there are five people in the pot and a total of $60.00. On the river, everyone checks to you. In a $1-$4-$8-$8 game, you may well want to risk $8.00 to win the $60.00, even if you have nothing. This type of bet only needs to succeed one out of seven times (assuming there is an average of at least $56.00 -- 7 x $8.00 -- in the pot each time) for it to be profitable; but even if you do get called, remember the "advertising" factor.

Since we are discussing bluffing, what about calling someone who you suspect is bluffing? There is a poker adage that poor players -- PokerPigeons -- call too many hands pre-flop, post-flop and turn, but don't call enough hands on the river. On the other hand, the good players -- PokerSharks -- tend to fold more often on the early streets but call relatively more hands on the river.

Now, in that same $1-$4-$8-$8 game, suppose you have 2 kings and the flop comes Q-10-7. The turn is a 3, and the river is an ace. The pot is $60.00. Someone bets ahead of you. It's now your turn to declare. Do you call? The answer is, all things being equal, yes. Maybe the bettor has an ace, or even K-J, but you should call because now you are risking $8.00 to win $68.00. You only need to be right one in eight times for this to be profitable over the long run. The pot odds justify a call, even if you are sure that you are beaten. After all, if your opponent is bluffing and you don't call, it would cost you $68.00; on the other hand, calling when he is bluffing will net you $68.00.

* * *

If you are never bluffed out of a hand,
that means you are calling too often.

238

Advanced Strategies for Texas Hold'em

After you have mastered the basic strategies discussed above, there are two advanced strategies you might consider on occasion to enhance your hourly win rate. Both of these involve playing deceptively. But, before you attempt these, be sure that you have become skilled in the basic strategies.

In the first situation, you have a small-to-medium pair (up to eights) in a moderately loose game. Someone raises and the strategy is to reraise; i.e., "three-bet" the hand as if you have a pair of aces or kings. If an ace or a king flops, the play is to aggressively bet it out, never allowing anyone to take the lead. Let your opponents think you have the aces (or kings) -- perhaps a set. If the flop is 10-7-5 and someone bets, you raise. You must bet on the turn and the river, no matter what. Be careful with this strategy. If you use it, do so only on rare occasions.

A second advanced strategic gambit concerns those undesirable small connected suited hands that you have been warned against. Sometimes you can play these hands if you are the big blind and no one raises; then check the flop and raise the turn, no matter if you have no pair and no draw. Do this only if there are no overcards on the board (e.g., 3-4-6) or when the board is paired (e.g., K-K-7). The idea is to convince your opponents that you limped in with a weak hand, then either made a straight (in the first scenario) or happened to have the third king (in the second).

These advanced strategies are presented only for your interest and to make you think about the concept of deception -- how to "fool" your opponents. You do not need these types of strategic plays to be a winning hold'em player. Use them sparingly and in only the right situations.

Deception and stealth may win you one extra pot per session, but good self-control and the basic strategies will make you a winning player for a lifetime.

* * *

Life is not risk-free if you want to accomplish anything.
-- John Glenn, Astronaut and U.S. Senator

Patience and Perseverance. . .
If you think you have had it tough, consider this:

When this man was 22 years old, he went into business and failed. At age 23, he ran for his state legislature and lost. The next year, at age 24, he again failed in business. When he was 26, his sweetheart died, and he suffered a nervous breakdown the next year. He ran for office and was defeated at ages 34, 39, 46, 47, and 49.

Yes, he had it tough and seemed to be destined to be a loser. But patience and perseverance can pay off:

At age 51, Abraham Lincoln was elected the President of the United States!

CHAPTER SIX --
THE PSYCHOLOGY OF POKER

by Dr. Daniel E. Abrams, Ph.D. in Clinical Psychology and Poker Professional

Psychology is the study of human behavior and its relationship to feelings and thoughts. It is concerned with a person's behavior as related to his mental processes. The psychological makeup of a poker player can strongly influence whether or not he is a winner. One can apply the understanding of this psychology to the fundamentals of winning poker. Why do some people win consistently while others fail to do so? The difference largely can be explained on the basis of psychological characteristics.

Poker is a game of logic and reasoning, but emotions often dictate decisions. This is true at all levels of the game, at low stakes as well as high stakes games For example, every poker player knows the "high" of winning a big pot and the "low" of a really bad beat. Great players know how to integrate logical decisions with their emotions.

> *This chapter deals with the emotions and other psychological characteristics that affect one's success in playing the game of poker.*

Five Key Factors

There are five key factors to being a winning poker player. We will describe these and then discuss psychologically-related issues in some detail. Our objective is to help you become a better poker player, and a consistent winner!

> **Five Key Factors —**
> *Poker players who possess the first four factors are winning players. Those who possess all five are the best!*

(1) Self-Control and Discipline

It is important to be able to control your losses and take your wins. *How many times have I witnessed players having a great rush and jumping ahead $1,500 or $2,000 or even more. But then, the rush ends (as they always do) and the player is soon back to even. Soon after, he walks away a loser, lamenting his poor fortune and saying to himself, "Why didn't I stop when I was ahead?"* A player in control knows when to quit and knows when to keep playing, and has the discipline to make the right decision and act accordingly.

It is much easier to play well when you are winning than when you are losing. That's because when you win, you don't feel angry, frustrated, or stressed out. Of course, the inverse also applies. *It is always interesting to observe a fairly good player deteriorate in his play after he loses a tough hand because he allows his emotions to take over, losing his discipline and self-control.*

(2) Knowledge of the Basic Poker Rules and Strategies

You can learn the Basic Poker Rules and Strategies from this book. Study them. Another effective way to develop good poker skills is by watching the best players and emulating them. *(If you are properly using the Basic Poker Rules, you will sit out many more hands than you play, and therefore have ample opportunity to observe the other players at your table.)* You can also try out different strategies and see how they work -- like learning on the job.

(3) Aggressiveness

Good poker players are aggressive. It is important to "make a statement" to the other players that you are to be respected or even feared. The more you can intimidate your opponents, the more likely you will win. That's because you will have bigger pots when you are ahead and they will have smaller pots when they are ahead. This is overly simplistic, but the point is important and worth restating: ***If your opponents are afraid to bet because you might raise, that puts them at a big disadvantage.***

(4) Ability to "Read" Other Players

Poker is an adversarial game; it's you against them. If you watch the players carefully, and understand a little about psychology, you can learn to "read" them. After all, if you could see their hole cards, wouldn't you be in a position to make better decisions? If you know when they will bet, when/what hands they would raise on, and when they would fold, you can well see how this would help you to maximize your profits.

(5) Creativity

Creativity is a fifth factor, which is not really critical in being a winner, but it does help. As noted above, the predictability of your opponents is very useful to you. By the same token, your unpredictability makes you tougher to beat. Creativity permits you to accomplish that end.

* * *

Important Personality Characteristics

Why is it that some people can win at their favorite level and others never will? The difference is not always about intelligence, experience, or strategy. The difference can be explained on the basis of personality characteristics.

• Emotions are Important

Poker is a game of logic and reasoning, where emotions should not, but often do, dictate decisions. *(I have found this to be true even in higher limit games.)* As noted above, every poker player knows the "high" of a big pot being pushed to him and the "low" of a really bad beat. But, beyond that emotion, what does it mean to you when you win or lose a hand? Did you play it "right?" Did you make a mistake in judgment? Do you have the insight to realize when you make a mistake and know why? How do you interpret the final event of winning or losing? Are you proud of yourself for winning? If you lost the hand, are you frustrated? Feel like a loser? Feel defeated? Stupid?

Inadequate? Angry? Do you want revenge? A winning poker player does not let these emotions control his playing. A winning poker player learns from his mistakes while keeping his emotions under control.

• Money Management

Everyone who understands the game even a little agrees that it is important to manage your stake; i.e., limit your losses, take your wins, and never play in a game without sufficient $ backing. However, the ability to do this from a psychological perspective, is very complicated. For most players there are two times when it is especially difficult to leave the game and stop playing: (1) when you are losing; and (2) when you are winning.

Why is this? When you are winning, you feel good, happy, gratified, successful, and you don't want these feelings to stop. You want this "high" feeling to continue, so you keep playing. When you're $50 ahead you want $100. When you're $500 ahead you want $1,000. Right? And you fully expect to keep winning. So you play on -- and end up losing your profit and maybe even your buy-in. *How many times have I seen a player do this?*

Now, consider the opposite: When you are losing, you feel frustrated, angry, depressed, maybe even inadequate. When people feel this way, they tend to do things to cope with those feelings. They react. If you're playing basketball and losing, trying harder or playing more aggressively might help. But in poker, does trying harder make people play better poker? Usually not. Even if they do play better, there is no guarantee they will win. Poker is one of the few "sports" where you can play a hand perfectly and still lose to someone who plays the hand all wrong. *What a great game it is!*

• Patience: Do You Have It?

Patience is a good quality to have. Right? There are players who are very bright, can read cards well, are very aggressive, know all the basic poker rules and strategies, and yet have no hope of winning at poker in the long run. They lack the ability to WAIT -- patience!

As noted in Basic Poker Rule No. 3, you must be patient in waiting for the cards that are appropriate to permit you to make the investment to stay in on the opening round of betting. Otherwise, you are destined to be a losing poker player in the long run.

Can you learn patience? Patience is not a natural instinct; but it can be learned. For some people, it may be easier than for others.

Someone once approached me and asked me to help him become a better poker player. I said okay, and we sat down with a deck of cards. I told him that I wanted him to throw away every hand until he was rolled up. I bet him that he couldn't do it. He said he could. After about 30 hands, he couldn't stand it any longer and said he didn't want to continue. It was too boring. "Okay," I said, "then throw away every hand until you start with a pair of aces." He seemed happier with this new arrangement. But, after the first 20

246

hands without a pair of aces, he gave up. "I'll never get a pair of aces," he exclaimed. I told him our lesson was over.

Some people have, or can develop, the needed patience. Can you? If you desire to be a winning poker player, it is essential that you learn to be patient.

• Selective Aggressiveness

Another important "trait" is aggression. A poker player needs to have "selective aggression." Why can some players do this and others can't?

I was teaching my girlfriend how to be aggressive. She plays $1-$5 stud and, like many others, liked to throw in her $1.00 after the first three cards to see the fourth. I said to her in our practice sessions that I wanted her to raise every hand. She argued that this would be dumb. I insisted. By nature, she is a sweet, good-natured person -- much better liked by others than I am. She is not aggressive by character. So, she couldn't learn to be selectively aggressive until she could first learn just to be aggressive.

• Control Your Emotions

Poker is a complicated game of social interaction. Great players know how to integrate logical decisions with their emotions. It is not a bad thing to feel lousy when you lose. It is a bad and usually very costly thing to allow your emotions to dictate how you play. Great players have "insight" into themselves and know how to apply their psychological strong suits in order to win money.

Can I Control Myself?

Physiologically, our brain is separated into parts controlling thought, reason and judgment (called the cerebral cortex), and parts controlling emotions. Man has the most developed cerebral cortex, which distinguishes him from other species. The emotions (or impulses) that you feel motivate you to do things, i.e., act or react.

When we are angry, for example, we want to strike out at the things or persons that have injured us. Impulses (emotions) interact with rational thought, and both contribute to one's behavior. It is important to understand the degree to which each person's behavior is affected by his emotions and thought. Some individuals' behavior is impulse-driven, while others are able to almost completely control their urges and make all their decisions based on rational thought. This is significant because emotions are not rational; and rational actions are important in playing winning poker. Emotion is an urge or impulse that tends to have only the goal of expression without any regard for the possible consequences. When experienced without adequate control in a poker game, this can be devastating to the player.

If you are such an individual whose behavior is heavily influenced by your emotions rather than your thinking, you will almost certainly be a losing poker player. Learn to control your emotions -- or don't play poker. *(Think about this.)*

The control of our emotions originates in early childhood. Since psychology began studying this issue, theorists have argued how much of the propensity for emotional control is innate and how much is learned. Almost all agree, however, that it is a combination of both genetic and learned factors that dictate whether one acts emotionally or logically. Each person has a different natural or inborn tendency toward emotional control. Then, as we grow, we learn how to control or not control these urges.

Consider the familiar emotion of anger. What happens to a child when he gets mad? Is he allowed to express his anger in any way? If the child throws a tantrum, do his parents stand by and watch or do they try to exercise control? In a healthy childhood, the child is allowed to feel angry, but must learn how to express this anger in an appropriate way; e.g., by verbal expression, by striking a pillow, or through play. The child in this context, then, learns he is allowed to feel anger, but that its expression must be appropriate. The child thus learns to be in control of his natural emotion of anger.

This is exactly the same lesson one must bring to the poker table. It is perfectly okay to become angry when you lose a big hand. The key issue is whether this anger has an appropriate release -- or does it lead to behavior which is destructive to your bankroll.

There are at least three good ways to express the anger that you may feel at the poker table.

(1) Leave the table and go for a walk.

(2) Learn to scream to yourself (not aloud).

(3) Use your anger to become more determined and tougher -- and patiently wait for your opportunity to exact "vengeance" later by playing a hand well and winning the money of your adversary.

• Control, Control, and More Control

Of all the skills required of a good poker player, control is the most important. What does "control" mean? It means many things. A "controlled player" sets goals for himself and sticks with them. His decisions are not affected by lucky or unlucky streaks. He starts with a limit as to how much he is willing to risk playing poker.

Most poker experts recommend that you should have a "stake" of 200 times the maximum bet of the game you play. For example, if you play $20-$40 stud, you would need a stake of 200 times $40, or $8,000. This $8,000 must be money that you don't need for paying your rent, food, clothing or other necessities of life. Preferably, you should keep this money separate from your other money. This $8,000 stake theoretically should provide the good player enough capital so that he can ride out a bad streak without going broke.

In order to have self-control, it is essential that you keep track of your play. *Some people advocate keeping track by the hour, but I personally don't believe this is necessary.* Get yourself a ledger, and every time you play write down the particular game; e.g., $20-$40 stud, the date, how long you played and the outcome (+$200 or -$150, for example). You cannot accurately assess yourself unless you keep track of your wins and losses.

Keeping track can be painful. Many people start this process, but when they go on a bad streak, they quit keeping track. It is just too painful for them to keep writing losses in their ledger. But it is necessary if you want to be in control of your poker playing.

As a rule of thumb, when you can beat your game 65 to 70 percent of the time, you are ready to advance to the next level (assuming you have the necessary finances to increase your stake).

As you know, luck is a factor in poker playing, so you cannot determine your ability based on the short term. It really takes many sessions, perhaps three to five years, to find out how good you are.

By way of illustration, I was playing $20-$40 Texas hold'em against a very poor player. He was on a lucky streak and was about $1,500 ahead. He bragged to me that he had won 17 times in a row. If this were true (and it is possible he lied, but I'll give him the benefit of the doubt), then most likely he is severely deceiving himself in terms of his poker skill and his future. If one would check back with him in three months, or six months, or three years later, he will most probably be overall a loser -- if he kept track.

It is important to remember that good play may not be rewarded in the short run, but it is almost always rewarded in the long run.

Another important element of control is setting goals and limits for individual sessions. Learn how to take a win and leave the game while you are ahead. *Sometimes I might walk away a $25 winner after just three hours of play. It still counts as a winning session.*

Poker experts often disagree on when to decide to leave the game. Money limits are a much better criterion than time limits. *(By the way, you should never start to play when you have only a short amount of time available -- like you have to leave for the airport in half an hour.)*

But, what goal should you set to win when you sit down to play? A suggested basic goal is to double your buy-in. *Incidentally, my buy-in for $20-$40 is usually $500. For $40-$80, it is $1,000. So, in a $20-$40 game, if I am ahead $521.00 after five minutes, or six hours, I will probably cash in. I have never regretted cashing in a winner. Quite likely, I might occasionally miss out on that fantastic rush; but never end up a loser when you have a nice win.*

Remember, you are learning self-control. The decision to continue playing is a complicated one and includes such factors as: "How do I feel mentally and physically?" "Am I playing well?" "Is the game good?"

Now, what about limits for losing? As a general rule, never lose more than you can win in one session. *My usual loss limit at the $20-$40 level is $1,000; at $40-$80, it is $2,000. If you play $1-$5 it might be about $100, but not more than $200.*

When you are in control, you are able to take a loss and leave. No matter how great a player you are, you must accept that some days it will just be impossible to win even if you play every hand perfectly. *(That's just the nature of the game.)*

Another element of self-control is maintaining control of your emotions. Does the way you play change when you lose? When you are frustrated, do you play more hands? Do you become "unglued" and go "on tilt?" Do frustration, anger and stress affect your decision-making? For the majority of poker players, they do.

Control is often considered the most important factor in successful poker play. For many people, it is a difficult thing to develop. Some people play many years and never learn control. They are the ones who will be losers. *Don't let it be you.*

• Patience, Patience, and More Patience

The most important decision you will ever make in any game of poker is whether to play the hand after you have seen the starting cards. You are faced with this decision in every poker hand you will ever play. Probably over 90 percent of poker players err in the direction of playing too many hands. This is because they are eager to engage in battle and the process of waiting has no <u>apparent</u> financial gain. *("You can't win if you don't play," they believe. But, be assured, you will save $ if you don't lose!)*

The first thing to notice when you sit down at the table is how many hands each opponent plays. The best player usually is the one who plays the least number of hands. When this type of player plays a hand, he must be respected. You must look at this player very differently than the one who plays the most hands. The latter player is harder to read, but is to be less respected.

"How many hands should I play?" This is a difficult question to answer. The easy answer is that you must learn to be particular about which hands to play, and learn how to make good first decisions. There are many factors to determine this first decision, which are discussed in the

Basic Poker Rules (Chapter 2). In any case, your goal, as a winning player, is to learn patience. How do you do this? You sit and wait. Keep track of how many hands you have <u>not</u> played, especially when things are going badly. Get mad, get stubborn, get determined — but always be patient. *(My personal record is 18 consecutive hands without playing one. I am proud of this. What is your record?)*

> *If, on average, you are playing 50 percent, even 25 percent, of the hands dealt, you are playing too many.*

With regard to patience, some players may argue, "If I play too few hands, I'll miss some very big wins." They usually tell a story where they threw away a marginal or borderline hand, only to later see that it would have been a big winner. This "I-would-have-won" position is dangerous. It is true that not playing borderline-quality hands will sometimes lead to missing a "big one;" but, remember, success in poker must be judged over the long run and not by the results of any one hand.

Winning poker has to do with probability. You are trying to increase your chances of winning in the long term. Watch the borderline (or marginal) hands that you threw away and notice how many times you would have lost a "big one," instead of winning. This will encourage you to maintain self-control and patience.

There is an argument that loose players make to defend themselves and justify their way of playing. They say, "If I play too few hands, no one will ever call me when I have a great hand." Not true! Most players pay little attention as to how others play their hands. If you fold ten hands in a row, and then play one, you would think they'd all give you credit for a good starting hand. A few -- the PokerSharks -- will, but most poker players will not. They are busy looking at their own hands and not thinking much about what you might have. So, while the patient player might get a few less calls when he raises, this factor is far outweighed by how often the loose player will lose in the long run. Learn to have patience in order to be a winner.

• Selective Aggression and Intimidation

Many years ago I was playing in a $20-$40 seven-card stud game in California. It was a good game; that is, there were three poor players and four decent ones at the table. The pots averaged $400-$600. I was slightly ahead for the session and waiting patiently for a big hand.

One of the poor players went broke and soon after, a new player entered the game. I didn't know him and watched with interest as he sat down. He "looked" like a competent poker player -- well groomed and dressed, and in his mid-50s. He bought in for $1,000, a large amount for this level of game. His first hand showed a 10 as his door card. He raised and two players called, myself included. The new player (let's call him Mr. X) bet out to the end. No one called, and he collected about a $350 pot.

The next hand Mr. X's door card was a king. Again he raised, no one called, and he won the ante. I wondered if he really had the best hand two times in a row. I also wondered if he would play every hand in the same way. The next hand, Mr. X had a queen as his door card. He raised again. This time I started with a pair of split sevens. I called, as did one other player. On the fourth card, I checked and Mr. X bet. The third player dropped out and I called. I had already decided to test Mr. X on the fifth card. It was time to find out if he really had queens. I checked, he bet and I raised. Not surprisingly, Mr. X threw his hand away and I won the pot with my pair of sevens.

Mr. X then changed his play. From that point on, he played very tightly and conservatively. He played another half-hour, won one additional pot and cashed out a $400 winner. After he left, I asked another player if he knew Mr. X. He told me that Mr. X played there occasionally and was known as a world-class stud player.

Mr. X had the philosophy that aggression and intimidation were the most fundamental skills of poker. When he sat down, he made a statement that he was the best and toughest player; and he "owned" the table. I have little doubt that Mr. X would have continued his aggression had I not stopped him with my mighty pair of sevens.

Now, this philosophy is not for everyone. It could well backfire for many players. But, Mr. X knew that he could intimidate most other players and used this knowledge to his best advantage.

Aggression and intimidation are necessary skills in most poker games and at most levels. It is important, however, to know when to apply this strategy and when not to. In very loose games, where every hand gets called to the end, raising every time and betting out will not work. In very tight games, it will usually lead to winning some antes and a small overall win. It works best in a game that falls somewhere between loose and tight.

It is necessary that your opponents have some fear of you. If they are afraid of your raise, they are much less likely to bet, even when they have the best hand. They are also less likely to raise you for fear of your reraise. This means that they will put more money in the pot when you are ahead and bet, and will put less money in the pot when they are ahead. This is an important ingredient for success.

What you should develop, therefore, is "selective aggression." This is the art of knowing when aggressive play will be effective and when it will not. In the example above, Mr. X used a particular variation on this theme. *Remember that if you are not an aggressive player, you probably are not an overall winner.*

Practice this aggressiveness whenever you play. See how it works. Figure out which players are most susceptible and which cannot be intimidated. If you occasionally err in the direction of over-aggressiveness, you still might benefit in the long run. After all, if you bet a weak hand, get called and lose the hand, every player at the table begins to doubt your credibility. The next time you have a strong hand, you are more likely to get called.

So, while aggression and intimidation in poker can't take the place of control, discipline, knowledge of strategy, and patience, it can be another valuable weapon in your "poker arsenal."

• Creativity

Just as it is desirable to understand how your opponents play, it is almost as important that they not be able to predict yours. It is, however, only the very advanced player who understands the advantage of being creative by varying his style of play. Even very good players tend to have a set and rather rigid regimen of play. That is, most players will play the same hand the same way each time. Now, if you are astute in your understanding and application of basic strategy, this consistency of play is a virtue. But, let's take it one step further. If you can vary how you play identical hands at different times, then you become unpredictable -- and that is to your benefit.

To elaborate on this important point, let's suppose you are playing in a pretty decent $10-$20 stud game. It is pretty decent because there are three poor players, three average players, and one good one. You are dealt a pair of jacks in the hole. One player calls before you and you raise. Two players call the raise. On sixth street, you make an open pair and bet. No one calls and the pot is pushed to you. You played correctly. Right? Well, let's say that ten hands later you are dealt another pair of pocket jacks. This time you don't raise, and there are three callers. On sixth street, you make an open pair and check, indicating your hand is weak. Someone else bets and you raise with your jacks-up. Your opponent calls. On the river you bet and he calls. Your jacks-up beats his nines-up. You are pushed a much bigger pot than in the first scenario.

Now, let's not get into an argument about which is the best way to play. In fact, it isn't even the outcome that is critical here. You could have lost either or both hands playing exactly the same way. What is crucial here is that you have become an unpredictable player. You have been creative. No one can "read" your hand based on how you play it. This is a big edge for you and leads to opponents making many more mistakes against you.

Consider a different typical example: You are playing $20-$40 Texas hold'em. It is a poor game -- very tight, with small pots. You are in fifth position and dealt two kings. You don't raise. Both blinds call and one other player raises. You and the two blinds call. The flop is 10-8-4, all different suits. You check and the raiser bets. The blinds fold and you call. The turn is a queen. You check; the raiser bets, and you raise. He reraises; you reraise and he calls. On the river another ten hits. You bet and your opponent calls. He turns over A-Q suited, and you win with your pair of kings. It worked out just right, didn't it? But some time later you are dealt kings again. What should you do? Should you slow-play it and try to trap someone? Probably not. Your opponents are less likely to be trapped a second time. So this time you raise. When you vary your play, your opponents cannot figure out what you have. They are confused by your creativity.

Poker is a game of mistakes! The idea is to let your opponents make more mistakes than you. Do whatever you can to ensure your opponents are more likely to make mistakes. When you can be creative in your play, it prevents others from playing as well as you do.

• Coping With Adversity

No matter how good, how well-disciplined, controlled, and clever you are, at some point you will still be tormented by a bad streak. These streaks happen to all poker players and it really is unavoidable. They often occur completely by surprise; there is no way to predict their onset. The bad streak may last a day, a week, perhaps a month, or even a year. During this streak, unlikely events will happen, resulting in your losing hand after hand that you "should have won." The important first question is: Are you, in fact, in a "bad streak," or are you just a "bad" player? If you have played for ten years and been a consistent winner for that period of time, you are probably a good, very good, or great player who is experiencing some bad luck.

I have heard of poor players who are simply lucky "all the time," but for now let's assume that a long win streak is reflective of your skilled play. So then you start losing. First, it's a week, then perhaps a month, then six months. This is most likely a bad streak. This may seem obvious, but it is not. That's because if you are not a skilled player but think you are, you will be unable to assess whether your change from winning to losing is simply due to a bad streak or if the odds have caught up with you.

Playing in a lively $20-$40 Texas hold'em game at The Mirage, I was dealt a pair of jacks. I was in fourth position and raised. All folded except one opponent. The flop came 3-7-10 unsuited. I bet and my opponent raised. Now, I knew this person to be a poor player. So what did I do? I raised back. He called. The turn was no help and the river was another 10. I bet and he called. He turned over 3-7 of clubs. He had flopped two pair and had been in the lead until the river. When I turned over my two jacks, he angrily commented that he was unlucky to lose, because the ten on the river gave me two pair. But was he "unlucky" to lose or not? The answer is no. Playing heads up with two small suited cards against a big pair is very poor poker strategy. But because he was such a poor player, he didn't have a clue about this. The point is that if this player complained of being on a "bad streak," it was not necessarily so. He was just a poor player who had lost a hand that he shouldn't have even played.

On the other hand, a day later a good player told me that he had played in a Texas hold'em game in which, within two hours, he lost five consecutive hands which he had started with a pair of queens or better. This was definitely bad luck and possibly part of a "bad streak."

The other point to remember, however, is that you don't know how long the streak will last. Your goal is to survive during this time and wait for it to end. Some very good players are not able to survive this streak and end up broke. Remember, if you are broke you are in no position to return to the game and wait for the turnaround. Winning poker is largely about probability; but, in the short-term, probability theory is not the law. The next time you start with a pair of aces and are heads-up against a player with 2-3 unsuited, just because the odds are in your favor doesn't mean you will win. And if the flop comes 4-5-6, and you lose a bunch, it doesn't mean that this same event will happen the next time you have aces. But it could. . .

Since bad streaks are unavoidable, they become a test of your poker-playing character. Almost every player goes into the game with the hope and expectation of winning. In fact, if you don't have this expectation you shouldn't be playing. But how can you continue to expect to win when you are on a bad losing streak?

First, you must ask yourself, "Why do I want to win?" and "What will losing mean to me?" These are two critical questions. Let's look at the first question. For some, winning is a financial necessity. These are the small number of people who play poker for a living. For most others, poker is recreation only. They are playing with money they don't really need for any other purpose. And, of course, there are many people within the continuum between these two extremes. Where are you?

In any case, for most poker players, winning or losing usually has other consequences besides financial ones. There are emotional consequences. Winning makes us feel good, successful, skilled, and perhaps even worthwhile. Losing can make us feel angry, depressed, and frustrated -- like a "big loser." This leads to a loss of self-worth. That is, to some degree, we begin to feel that we are losing because we are "a bad person." Now, in its worst form, this negative self-feeling can permeate one's life and even lead to thoughts of suicide. In addition, people seek reasons to explain things that happen to them.

It is our natural inclination to believe things that happen to us have a purpose or meaning. So, the losing poker player asks himself questions: "Am I being punished for something I did wrong?" "Am I losing because the Lord hates me?" "Am I losing because I was mean to my kids yesterday?" And so forth and so on. We try to find a reason; but, of course, there is none. The truth is that many things in this world just happen, without any reason or purpose. It is just chance playing its fickle game with our lives.

What should you do about a losing streak? One suggestion is to take a break. If you are doing badly, skip playing poker for a few days, or a few weeks. It helps to "clear your brain" and to keep you in control. A second suggestion is to go into a smaller limit game than you ordinarily play. Most players in a bad streak make the costly and stupid mistake of moving to a higher-stakes game. *You should move up in limits when you are doing well, not when you are on a losing streak.* Thirdly, you might switch to a different game. If you are as good or almost as good at some other game, try it for a while. Finally, change your strategy. On a bad streak, you should play more tightly (fewer hands). *On the other hand, on a good streak, it's okay to play a few more hands; perhaps, go in on some marginal hands that you would not have played normally.*

How do you maintain a positive attitude when you are doing poorly? Remember that everyone goes through these streaks and they always end. Now, we don't know how long the streak will last, but you must constantly remind yourself that your day will come. The key is to still be around when it happens.

• Self-Image

All people have self-image, or self-concept. This is the way they perceive and evaluate themselves. Some refer to it as self-esteem. It is generally considered a positive personality attribute. This self-concept develops from an early age, during childhood. For some, it never changes; for others, it changes a great deal over a period of years.

Each of us has a need to view ourselves in a positive way. We want to feel good about ourselves; this is a healthy need. We also want to feel that what we do is valuable and that we are successful, intelligent, etc. These same needs are brought to the table by each poker player.

Once at a $20-$40 seven-card stud game in a California casino, someone at the table made a comment about how poorly one of the players had played a hand. The person overheard the comment and reacted: "Oh, yeah, well I'm a lot better player than you are; ask anyone!" Then the other person asked the other players at the table who they thought was the best player. Do you know what happened? Each player said that he thought he was the best player. Isn't that interesting? Could they all be the right? The fact is there were true differences in their abilities, but few could accurately see these.

* * *

How to Assess Your Opponents

Poker is, by its very nature, an adversarial endeavor. The purpose of the game is to walk away with more money than you sat down with, taking with you some of your opponents' money. In order to do this on a consistent basis, it is important that you know and "understand" the opposition. Toward this end, to the extent that you can, make use of tells. (*See Chapter 4.*) In addition, the following are some useful suggestions.

One of the first things that a PokerShark does when he sits down at a table is to study each of the opponents. This is especially desirable if you have not played with them before. Observe how much money each has in front of him. Players with short money usually play differently than those with an ample stash. It is also more difficult to bluff a player who probably will go all in during the hand. This particular player will likely be at a point where he says, "I'm going home anyway. I might as well see the last card." This is not a good scenario for an aggressive player who counts on opponents to be cautious and easily intimidated. How can you bluff someone out who is all in?

The second thing to notice about each player is his physical appearance. Does his posture, countenance, and general appearance suggest success or failure -- winner or loser? It's just an impression you might be able to glean. How do they stack their chips? This can be an important clue regarding what type of players they are: Very neat chip "stackers" tend to be more controlled and tighter than players who have "messy" stacks of chips. Note each opponent's general attitude. Is he having fun? As a general rule, more serious, intent-looking players tend to be more skilled than those who are smiling and engaged in idle conversation. Of course, this could be an act. However, it's not likely that players are "acting" in low-to-intermediate level games. *(What you see is pretty much what you get!)*

The person who plays one in seven hands must be judged very differently than someone who plays every other hand. The former is likely to be a PokerShark; the latter is more likely to be a PokerPigeon. *Of course, you want to play against the PokerPigeons!*

Notice how each hand is played. While it is considered poor protocol to ask to see a player's hand if it isn't shown, watch carefully the ones that are turned up. Pay special attention to whether the player is aggressive or not. Is he someone who likes to take the lead and keep it? Or does he prefer to sit back and call? These players must be played very differently. For instance, a check-and-raise strategy will only work if you are relatively sure that your opponent will bet.

Categorize your opponents by rating each one at your table. What is the quality of their play? A rating system can be used to do this. One approach is to rate players on a one-to-five scale -- five being the best, a PokerShark. *You'll be surprised how quickly you can learn to do this when you practice.* Use this scale freely. As the game progresses, you may revise your assessment. In other words, if a level-one player plays a hand well, move him up a notch or two. It helps to rate your opponents as well as yourself. Let's assume that you think you are a level-three player (about average). You sit down at a game and begin to observe the other players. After about fifteen minutes you determine that there are four level-three players, two level-four players, and one level-five player. In other words, there are no players with a rating lower than yourself. Your conclusion should be that you are playing in the wrong game. You are sitting at the wrong table. . .

On the other hand, what if there are four level-three players (same as yourself), one level-four (slightly better than yourself, and two level-one players? Now you have found a game that you can beat *(assuming the cards will cooperate)*. During the game, you would prefer to be in situations where you are playing against two poor players (or at least one) and the best player is not in the hand.

On one occasion when I was playing in a game of Texas hold'em against a level-one type — basically any two starting cards looked good to him — I was dealt a pair of queens. I raised and two other players, including the level-one type, called. After the flop I bet and only the level-one type called. I bet on the turn and he called. The river card was an ace. Now, a level-one player will call any hand to the end if he has any possibility of winning. I knew this man would call to the river with an ace and any other card. So, I checked. He chuckled and turned over A-9 unsuited. The dealer pushed the pot to him. Lady Luck had been very kind to him and unkind to me.

Is it possible for a game to be <u>too good</u>? That is, would you play in a game with five level-one players and four level-two players if you were a level-four type?

In such a game, the good player will experience many more bad beats. That's because a starting hand of a pair of aces in seven-card stud or Texas hold'em is not a favorite against five opponents no matter what cards they start with. But, when you win a pot in such a game, it will be a big one. *So, I like games where there are the most number of poor players, recognizing that there will be greater variance in my stack — ups and downs like a roller-coaster ride.*

You can use this rating system to decide if you are playing in the "right" game. If there are too many superior players, it's not the game for you.

In the sport of football, each team spends many hours watching films of its next opponent to see how it plays. This helps the team develop its strategy for the upcoming game. As a poker player, you can do a similar thing (watch how he plays), but you have one advantage: If you think your opponent is too tough, you can walk away without any penalty.

* * *

Enjoy your life as you have it.
--Dani Epstein (age 7)

Moving Up

Most people who start to play poker in casinos begin at the lowest limits. In Las Vegas today, this means $1-$5 (or $1-$4) limit stud and $3-$6 limit Texas hold'em. It is human nature, however, to want to play for higher stakes. So, soon after starting to play, most people move up to the next level. This is particularly true if your initial sessions are successful. You think, "This is easy money. Since I won $40 playing $1-$5 stakes, I could win $100 playing $5-$10." So, greed is one of the prime factors in most player's decision to move up to a higher stakes game.

There are two other psychological factors that may be involved. One is boredom. After playing at one level, the money seems to lose significance. The pots, which originally may have seemed large, now seem small. The challenge disappears and it becomes harder and harder to be patient. So, to increase the excitement, many poker players want to play for higher stakes. They scout the tables at the next level, and the pots look inviting.

Ego is another factor in the decision to "rise" to the next level in poker. People want to "see" themselves as good players. They think, "I'm as smart as the people playing $5-$10; why shouldn't I play against them?" They reason that since they are good enough to "beat" their current game, they should be able to "beat" the game at the next level, too.

As a matter of fact, these three factors are not the correct ones for making such an important decision: whether or not to advance to the next level in poker. It is desirable to be more practical and realistic. . .

No wife can endure a gambling husband unless he is a steady winner. -- Lord Dewar

The Key Factors in Deciding to Move Up

First and foremost, from a practical standpoint, you must consider the "money" factor. As noted previously, you should have a bankroll of 200-300 times the maximum bet. This is $1,000 to $1,500 in a $1-$5 game; but it is $2,000 to $3,000 at the $5-$10 level. This is a big difference. Ask yourself if you are prepared to risk/invest this "kind" of money in the game of poker.

Secondly, you should be able to "beat" the game you are playing 65 to 70 percent of your sessions. People who know this sometimes think that if they win seven out of the last ten times they play at one limit level, they now are ready to move up. This is wrong. Ten sessions is not a large enough sampling to determine if you're really better than the game or just had some pretty good luck. One hundred or so sessions would be more suitable. If you win 65 to 70 times out of 100 sessions, you meet this second criterion for moving up. (Note: Playing twice a week, it will take about one year to be able to make this determination.)

Thirdly, as a general rule, you will find that the players are more skilled with each level that you move up. *There are, of course, exceptions. Some people play very poorly at $40-$80 level poker. In fact, a small percentage of these players are worse than players at the $1-$5 level. Strange, but true.* In general, if you are the best player at $1-$5, you might only be an average player at $5-$10. If this is the case, it will be more difficult to win at the higher level. And then the game of poker might become much less

270

interesting and less exciting, and more frustrating for you. Be prepared to compete against more skilled players -- provided you have the bankroll and your winning statistics show that you are ready to move up.

Expect Differences When You Move Up

There are notable differences in poker games depending on the stakes. For example, there is more raising and bluffing at higher levels than at lower ones. Ante or blind stealing is much more frequent in intermediate and high level games, but insignificant in small games. Also, almost certainly, better hands are found at the river in lower- level hands than at higher stakes games because more players are prone to chase, hoping to make their hands.

> *There are players who are never satisfied with the level which they are playing. It's as if they want to move up until they find the level they can't beat.*
>
> *(Sort of like the Peter Principle: A person advances to his level of incompetence.)*

The decision as to what level of stakes you should play is multi-faceted. It is important that you make that decision based on logical and practical factors and not emotional ones. When you find a level at which you are successful, enjoy your success. Don't be in a hurry to play with the "big boys" — at least until you fully satisfy the three criteria discussed above.

* * *

Don't Blame the Dealer

In one sense, the dealer is responsible for what happens to you when you play poker. After all, is he not mixing and shuffling the cards, and dealing them to you? So, if the dealer gives you a worse hand than your opponent and you lose your money, is it not the dealer's "fault?"

When "bad" things happen, it is natural to want to blame someone. *Think about this for a minute.* When you experience a bad beat, whom can you blame? You have three choices: yourself, your opponent, or the dealer. Most people prefer to blame someone other than themselves. This leaves your opponent and the dealer. Blaming the other player and becoming abusive to him could be dangerous. After all, the other player could abuse you back. Or, if he is prone to violence, might even try to assault you physically. *(I once had an experience where another player threatened me during a game and said he would "take care" of me later in the parking lot).* The easiest and safest target for a player's anger or abusive language is the dealer. And so, some players tend to blame the dealer for their losses. *(Apparently, it doesn't occur to them that it may be just the "luck of the draw.")*

Some poker players have dealers they dislike and others they like. Some players will actually stop playing when certain dealers come to their table. Others will actively seek out those dealers who have been "good" to them in the past, and dealt them winning hands. It's human nature. In fact, even some very good players have developed superstitions about different dealers.

An important point here is that the dealer must be viewed by all players as an objective, but interested, third party in the competition among the players. The dealer should not be extra friendly to one player. When a dealer does this, it makes the other players feel less favored. This can lead to players becoming angry at the dealer when they lose a hand. It is especially important that dealers show no emotion when they push a pot to the winner. A brief smile, even a word, can be inciting to the loser of the hand. A dealer must be careful to never communicate any favoritism or bias to any of the players.

Dealing poker is a tough job. *I have often felt sympathy toward a dealer who received abuse from an unruly player.* But it is critical that the dealer do his job in a professional manner and show control over his own emotions. In this way, he will be able to conduct a faster, more efficient game, and also be less subject to negative language from the players at the table.

In any case, abusive treatment directed toward a dealer or another player should never be tolerated at the poker table.

* * *

A Mistake in Poker is Not Always a Mistake

Everyone who has played poker has had the opportunity to mourn incorrect decisions. It is human nature that we sometimes make mistakes in all endeavors, and poker playing is no exception. It happens to the best players in the world.

How do we define a mistake in poker? The most common way is based on outcome. An example of this would be throwing away a hand that was really the best one. A second example would be not raising when a well-timed raise would have resulted in a win. The less skilled you are as a player, the more likely you are to define a mistake based on the outcome.

A good player knows that this type of post-mortem analysis is both self-destructive and specious. It is self-destructive because it makes you feel badly about yourself. You castigate yourself for not raising or for throwing away the winning hand. This results in less confidence as a poker player and may affect your play in subsequent hands. Additionally, this type of retrospective analysis is false. Let's say, for example, you start with a pair of sixes in a $1-$5 seven-card stud game. A man with a jack up raises to $5.00 and you hesitate. You notice that one other six is already out, and your kicker card is only a trey. You *(quite properly)* throw your hand away rather than call the raise. Someone else calls and you get to see that your next card would have been the case six, giving you trips. You curse yourself for not staying in. You say to yourself that you should have stayed and you count this as a mistake. But is it? Absolutely not! Your lay down of the "practically-dead" sixes against a most likely pair of jacks was the prudent and correct decision. The point is that you didn't make a mistake in this situation.

• How do we properly define a mistake in playing poker?

> As a general rule, a mistake in poker is not knowing and/or not playing according to probability odds.

Let's consider the above example: The player with the two sixes is more than a 2-to-1 underdog against two jacks. Does it make sense to be betting even money when the odds are 2-to-1 against you? Of course not.

Now, let's take another example: You are playing in a $20-$40 hold'em game. You are dealt K-J. The flop is K-6-4 unsuited. You bet with a pair of kings, and get two callers. The turn card is a 10. You bet and one opponent raises. You put him on a set of sixes, fours, or tens -- three-of-a-kind. There is $270.00 in the pot. What do you do? If you are correct in your analysis of his hand, then you are drawing practically "dead;" i.e., there is no river card except another king that could win you the hand. Your card odds are very poor relative to the pot odds. The correct decision is to fold. Now, let's say that you do drop out, and the river card happens to be a jack. Both remaining players check. Then the raiser turns over 10-6. Oh my! You would have won with your K-J. So you tell yourself that you "should have" called his raise. Absolutely not! You played correctly and should applaud yourself for your analysis, discipline, and control. You considered the probability odds in making your decision, and played your hand accordingly.

Now, how about a more difficult example. You are playing $20-$40 hold'em and are dealt a pair of 10s. You are in sixth position, and there is a raise ahead of you. You make it three bets ($60.00). Two opponents call. The flop is 3-4-5, with the latter two cards spades. You bet and both opponents call. The turn is the 10 of spades. Now you have three 10s! You bet and the first opponent raises to $80.00. What do you do? An aggressive player would raise back, since there are a number of hands that would justify a raise by your opponent that still could not beat your trip tens. The conservative player would call, putting his opponent on a flush. Let's say that he does have the flush. Why do you call when you believe you are behind? There is $510.00 in the pot. The odds of your winning the hand on the river are about 4-to-1 against you. (Of the remaining 46 unseen cards, there are 10 cards which would win the hand for you my making a full house or better: three 3s, three 4s, three 5s, and one 10 for four-of-a-kind.) It is, therefore, well worth $40.00 to try to win $510.00 -- pot odds of over 12-to-1. This would be the equivalent to someone offering you 3-to-1 odds on a coin toss. In addition, if you happen to be wrong in your analysis of your opponent's hand, there is still the possibility that your three 10s is the best hand. This makes a call on the river imperative even if you don't fill up.

Good players know the importance of calculating and responding to pot odds. That is the proper basis for making a decision. If the decision turns out to be wrong, it is not a mistake. It is only the best decision at the time that turned out to be wrong.

Many times in life we are faced with difficult decisions. The reasonable way to make them is to calculate to the best of our ability all the possible outcomes and then choose the one that we determine is the most favorable to us. But, we all know that no one is infallible in the decision-making process. Remember this when playing poker.

The reasonable/rational decision does not always work out the way we hope, but that doesn't mean that next time we should make a less rational decision in the same situation.

* * *

Compulsive Gambling

Years ago, as a practicing psychologist, I provided counseling to many individuals who had gambling problems.

A "gambling problem" is behavior that interferes with the rest of a person's life. The gambling causes financial stress, personal-relationship problems, and perhaps even physical problems. In its worst form, gambling becomes the dominating force in a person's life and may lead to bankruptcy, divorce, or even suicide.

People with compulsive gambling problems cannot stop; after losing their initial buy-in, they will take out more money. When this money is gone, they will try to look for money elsewhere. They will use their ATM cards; and when their limit is reached, they will use their credit cards. After their credit cards are "maxed out," they will borrow money from anyone they can. They will use money they need to pay the rent, car payment or even food. Obtaining money with which to gamble becomes their primary objective.

Compulsive gamblers cannot believe their "bad luck." They almost always have a distorted sense of their ability. That is, they think that they are losing because they are extremely unlucky, rather than poor players.

The compulsive gambler needs the rush of the action. He craves it! When he is not gambling, he is thinking about gambling. This begins to affect his work. His work performance declines. He may take off work early so that he can go play. He may even call in sick so that he can go to gamble. More and more, gambling consumes his life.

His personal relationships suffer. If he is married, the gambling leads to major conflict with his wife. She wants to know where the money is. So the compulsive gambler begins to lie. He makes up excuses about the money. He tries to conceal his losses from her.

Even the compulsive gambler who is not married has all sorts of relationship problems. He misses a date with a girlfriend because he cannot leave the game. He stands up a friend for a basketball shoot-around. He fails to do a favor for his sister because he "doesn't have time."

Likewise, his relationships at work suffer serious consequences from this behavior. He may be passed up for a raise or promotion. He may receive warnings about his work performance. Ultimately, he may be fired!

He neglects his car -- until the defects force him to the repair shop; and then the repairs are more costly. Likewise he neglects the maintenance of his home -- and even of his own personal self. He has lost his self-esteem.

His personality changes. The losses affect his disposition. He is increasingly irritable and angry. He gets into more arguments with everyone. People see him as less dependable, less trustworthy. And he seems moody and "down" to others.

He can't sleep at night. He lays in bed going over in his mind the losses of the day. This sleep deprivation leads to more problems. He is more irritable and tired all the time; and he can't eat. Food becomes increasingly unimportant. He becomes physically ill.

Gambling as an addictive behavior is extremely difficult to treat. It is at least as difficult to overcome as compulsive eating, drug or alcohol addictions.

Compulsive gambling can take various forms. That is, the compulsive gambler may play poker, craps, horse racing, blackjack, video poker machines, or slots -- one or more of these. It is not the choice of game that matters, it's the way the compulsive gambler approaches the game.

One final thought:
Compulsive gambling is not exclusive to males.
The use of "he" to describe the gambler is for simplicity.
This addiction knows no sex, race, or age barriers.
It is an equal-opportunity addiction!
If you have this problem, go get some help.

Playing poker can be many useful things, including profitable. It is not, however, for those who can not control themselves. Think about it. . .

* * *

Some Oxymorons Just for Poker Players:

- Passive aggression
- Acting naturally
- Sweet sorrow
- Almost exactly
- Small crowd
- Working vacation
- Genuine imitation
- Found missing
- Terribly pleased
- Soft rock
- Pretty ugly
- Silent scream
- Definite maybe
- Now, then. . .
- Good grief

CHAPTER SEVEN --
MAKING AN ALLOWANCE FOR ANTES;
RECOMMENDATIONS FOR
TIPPING/SHOWING YOUR APPRECIATION

*Never underestimate the power of a kind word
or deed!*
>   -- H. Jackson Brown, Jr.; in *Life's Little Instruction Book*;
>   Rutledge Hill Press; 1991.

How Should Antes Affect Your Playing?

To some extent, playing winning poker as described in this book -- using the basic rules and strategies -- is best geared to no-ante or low-ante (relative to the size of the bets or the stakes) games. In no-ante, seven-card stud, each player gets three cards to look at <u>before</u> investing any money. On the other hand, most poker games, especially home games and those played in poker parlors, often require an ante: money (or chips) put into the pot <u>before</u> any cards are dealt. The ante does not have any effect on the use of the Basic Poker Rules, but it may affect some of our strategies.

> *Do not confuse the ante with the house's rake. These are separate and distinct from one another. As noted previously, the rake is that portion of the pot — usually a relatively small percentage or a fixed amount — that the house takes as its share to cover its expenses and provide a profit for its owners.*

Generally speaking, the higher the ante relative to the size of the bets, the less money you likely will net out at the end of the poker session. The ante may be likened to the overhead costs that a business must endure in order to stay in business. We can regard the ante as sort of a "head tax" — a charge or fee paid for sitting at the table and playing poker there. If 30 hands are dealt in an hour *(I have counted as many as 40 hands dealt in one hour),* and the ante is $0.50, then each player (including yourself) must pay $15/hour to play poker at that table. You will win some of the hands and collect the ante as part of the pot; however, the additional amount you collect will hardly make up for this "head tax."

- **The lower the ante relative to the size of the bets, the more it is to your advantage — when you play according to our Basic Poker Rules.**

- **Whenever possible, try to play in no-ante or, if necessary, low-ante games relative to the stakes.**

282

Do not regard the antes as insignificant. Strictly as an experiment, I kept track during a typical no-ante seven-card stud poker session in one of the hotels in Las Vegas: In 1.5 hours there were a total of 53 hands dealt at the table -- which was full almost the entire time. That corresponds to about 35 hands dealt per hour. Playing strictly by our rules, I folded, i.e., did not pay for the opening bet -- as per the third Basic Rule for Winning at poker -- in 38 of these 53 hands. Also, I would not have gone into the hand for an additional 6 hands except that I held the low upcard and hence was forced to open. In other words, out of a total of 53 hands, I was dealt just 9 that merited an opening bet. I won two of the hands during this period of time.

To bring this analysis into better perspective, assume this were an ante game and the ante was $1.00. That means I got an additional $7.00 in each pot I won -- from the antes paid in by the other players. Since I won two hands, the added "income" was $14.00. However, on the "debit" side, I would have had to ante a total of $53.00 ($1.00 ante x 53 hands dealt). Net income from the antes: a negative $39.00!

Many poker parlors do require an ante, and the house takes its rake right out of the antes before the cards are dealt. Playing in a typical $0.50-ante game of seven-card stud at the $3-$6 limit, there are approximately 24 hands dealt per hour of play. That means you would have to "shell out" $12.00 for each hour of play at that table. With a full table of eight players, the house takes out $3.00 as its rake; so there remains only $1.00 in the pot from the antes. (There would be just $0.50 if there were seven players in the hand.) With only one or two antes remaining in the pot, there is so little money in the pot that it makes sense to play your hands exactly as described in Basic Poker Rule # 3.

On the other hand, some changes in your playing are desirable in those ante games where there remains a sizable amount of money in the pot -- as, for example, in most home games or in poker games where players pay for "time." (A fee is charged by the house for letting the player participate in the game, and collected at regular time intervals -- rather than relying on a rake.) In such cases, the strategy described previously for raising with a high pair (Poker Strategy #1) is even more important. In the opening round of betting, you need not hold off if there are no opening bets before you; money is already in the pot. In such cases, you should bet high or raise (you have the best hand, hopefully) -- so long as there is the equivalent of three minimum bets in the pot (as stated previously) -- and you may "steal" the antes. In addition, because of the antes, the pot odds will be somewhat higher; this will enter into your calculation in weighing the chances of winning (card odds) versus the pot odds. This factor may make it more feasible to risk a call on an opening marginal hand, to draw another card -- i.e., to make an "investment" that would not be proper were there less money in the pot. (See Poker Strategy #2.)

* * *

Some Words of Wisdom -- Original source unknown
• *Experience is something you don't get until just after you don't need it.*
• *No one is listening until you make a mistake.*
• *To succeed in politics, it is often necessary to rise above your principles.*

284

Recommendations for Tipping

Most dealers receive little more than minimum wages.
They depend on their "tokes" to earn a living.

As an employee of the casino, the dealer's job is more than just to shuffle/mix and deal out the cards. In effect, he operates the game, and is responsible for making sure that the game moves along smoothly, with no cheating or problems, ensuring that all players are treated properly and fairly. The dealer must be impartial to all players involved and resolve any questions or conflicts -- sometimes with the help of the floorperson or cardroom manager. He must be capable of maintaining order and exercising good judgment at all times. It is the dealer's responsibility to see to it that each player follows all of the applicable regulations, and that all bets are properly made in the correct order and amount; and to distribute the pot to the winner(s) at the end of each hand, including any side pots. When a player goes all in, the dealer must determine the amount and control the money in the main pot and side pot. (Sometimes there are two or more side pots.) If a "new" player enters the game, a good dealer will make sure that he is familiar with the key regulations and customs, especially those regarding betting and raising; and may provide guidance to assist him.

Indeed, the dealer has a vital role in the play of the game. His alertness and skill are important factors in the success and enjoyment of the game.

Just like waiters in a restaurant, dealers in most poker rooms are paid little more than minimum wage by the casinos. Whether or not you agree, this is the way it is. Accordingly, players are expected (but certainly not required) to tip the dealer when winning a pot. *("Tokes" is a term often used in lieu of the word "tips.")* It's a way to show your appreciation for having been dealt the winning hand. Tipping the dealer after winning a pot is the standard practice -- except, of course, in home games where the players themselves take turns dealing.

The amount of the tip is left to the discretion of the player who wins the pot. In low-medium stakes games, tips are usually anywhere from $0.50 to several dollars, depending on the size of the pot. The more $ in the pot, the larger a tip one generally will push to the dealer -- while happily adding the chips into his stacks.

In an ante-game, a typical tip might be the size of the ante or perhaps somewhat more, depending on the size of the pot. In a no-ante game, the average tip might be about half the minimum bring-in bet -- again, more or less depending on the size of the pot. But there are no hard rules in this regard.

In high-stakes games which build huge pots, the tips can be much larger than in low-medium stakes games.

Some casinos feature a bonus for making a very high hand, or a "bad-beat" jackpot (where the player receives perhaps several thousand dollars if his monster hand -- say four-of-a-kind -- is beaten by a higher hand). In such cases the players receiving the bonus or jackpot will usually tip the dealer. For jackpots, the dealer's tip can be several hundred dollars.

Many players will adjust the size of the tip depending on the dealer's skill and attitude, and how well they have been doing at the table. Big winners are inclined to tip a lot better than losers. Some players tip lavishly.

Even if you are an overall loser in the game, it is customary to tip the dealer when you win a pot. It is appropriate to tip the dealer unless everyone folds on third street, or everyone in the hand has been checking from fourth street on -- so there is hardly any $ in the pot.

But bare in mind that excessive tipping will cut into your profits if you end the session ahead -- or add to your losses if you go home a loser.

In accepting a tip, the dealer will usually acknowledge it by saying, "thanks," and then often signal his acceptance by tapping the chip(s) or coin(s) on the table before placing it into his shirt pocket or the tray in front of him.

* * *

Don't be afraid to say, "I don't know."
Don't be afraid to say, "I made a mistake."
Don't be afraid to say, "I need help."
Don't be afraid to say, "I'm sorry."
Never compromise your integrity.
      -- H. Jackson Brown, Jr.; in *Life's Little Instruction Book;* Rutledge Hill Press; 1991.

CHAPTER EIGHT –
FOR SENIOR CITIZENS: PLAYING POKER
FOR FUN, $, AND GOOD HEALTH

We don't stop playing because we grow old;
we grow old because we stop playing.

-- George Bernard Shaw

How to Live Longer and Healthier by Participating
in Mentally and Physically Challenging Activities

I have saved this chapter for last; it offers me the unique opportunity to present my personal message based on first-hand experience that only other senior citizens can fully appreciate. *(You can judge my qualifications based on the fact that I was born November 9, 1926 in Boston, MA.)* Having taken up the game of poker on a fairly serious basis since my retirement from full-time employment in November 1991, I have been able to assess some of the unexpected benefits from playing the game of poker -- and experiencing the excitement and joy of becoming a winning poker player. *(I win approximately 75 percent of the sessions I play, and find myself doing better as I hone my own skills.)*

The message you are about to "hear" I have presented to a number of senior citizens groups and at an Elderhostel -- not counting professional organizations and a cruise ship which included many senior citizens. In fact, this message should serve the interests of those who are nearing retirement from their day-to-day chores of earning a living, as well as those already retired — a rapidly growing segment of our population.

First, before delving into the context of this chapter, allow me to offer a few words of wisdom based on personal experience and observations:

Never just retire from the work force.
It is important to retire <u>into</u> something.

In planning retirement, have activities — perhaps a hobby, a series of projects, travel plans — to keep you mentally and physically active after retirement from the day-to-day employment market. Join a health club for physical exercise or use its swimming pool. Retirement activities should also provide mental challenge to stimulate your mind.

For myself, poker has served as one means to achieve that end. I also teach an engineering course at UCLA, edit a technical newsletter, do consulting for government and industrial organizations, serve as an officer in a professional engineering society, and write a column in Poker Player newspaper — and very much enjoy my two very wonderful and beautiful granddaughters who I am teaching to be winning poker players as well as winners in the game of life! That's a mental challenge in itself. And I exercise regularly.

I don't know what I don't know. Teach me!
    -- Stuart Simon, poker expert, business consultant, and senior citizen

> **• What I discovered . . . was that people who are active and engaged in things they like were the ones who stayed healthy and lived longer and had better quality of life.**
> -- Norma Barzman, author and screenwriter

The game of poker provides the mental challenge and stimulation that leads to a healthy mind. The human brain is a part of our nervous system; it is the organ in our body that is responsible for thought and nerve coordination. Physically, it is enclosed within the skull, and consists of nerve cells and fibers, with blood carrying oxygen flowing through blood vessels and veins. It provides us with memory, and the ability to feel, think, perceive and reason.

> **• Mental exercises, like physical exercise, can help older people sustain and in some instances even improve their mental abilities.**
> -- Professor W. Warner Schaie, Penn. State University

According to Dr. William T. Greenough, Professor of Psychology and Chairman of the Program in Neurosciences & Behavioral Biology at the University of Illinois at Urbana-Champaign, "Mental exercise is a very good thing for the health of the brain. It's similar to the effect of physical exercise on the rest of the body. Older people who remain active . . . feel a continuing sense of purpose, and are motivated to depend on themselves and their own resources." Live an active rather than a passive life-style, he urges. You can do so by playing poker (or other mentally challenging game such as bridge) -- rather than spending "mindless hours staring at the television."

Dr. Martin A. Samuels, Chief of the Department of Neurology at Brigham and Women's Hospital, Boston. MA, has stated that "the brain enjoys a learning challenge and responds to it with increased activity that can carry over into other mental tasks. So if you keep on learning, your brain will, too." The mental activity spurs brain cells to "sprout" new connections called synapses. Thus, mental challenges as presented during the poker game, can be a key to slowing, perhaps preventing, the decline of intellectual capacity which once was considered inevitable during our aging process.

You Have A Choice. Decide Wisely. . .

Upon retirement, most of us have a choice. It's an important choice. We can elect either to accept

• Challenge and responsibility -- leading to being more alert, active, healthier, and living longer; or select
• Isolation -- leading to boredom, lack of intellectual challenge, and mental deterioration.

The choice is yours. If you elect the first and decide to play poker, then you should do so with the intent of becoming a winning poker player. *(This book has shown you how to accomplish that goal.)*

As an aside, while doing research for this chapter, I learned that sex helps mental health and boosts the immune system, helping to prevent colds and headaches. According to Dr. Alexander Mauskop, Director of the New York Headache Center (Ref. Bottom Line Newsletter; April 1, 2000), higher levels of immunoglobulin-A were produced by those who averaged two sexual encounters per week, protecting them against disease. These same people also reported fewer migraine headaches -- because sex releases hormones that prevent migraines! When I noted this finding at a talk to a senior citizens group, one "young woman" who I took to be in her late 60s, smiled coyly and commented: "So do you advise having sex while playing poker?" What could I respond?

There is yet another -- rather subtle -- benefit that senior citizens (others too) can derive from playing poker. I have observed that my ability to exert self-control or self-discipline has improved as I focused on this skill which is essential to winning at the game of poker. *(See Chapter 6.) That's an unexpected perquisite that has benefited my daily life away from the poker tables.*

For example, I have been able to apply my improved self-control to my desire to consume desserts at meals. Following my doctor's advice, I try to exercise more and eat less of the foods that are not good for me -- such as sweets. Case in point: My ladyfriend, Anita, and I were at an elegant social affair. After a delicious dinner, tables of desserts were brought forward: cookies, cakes and pies, and all flavors of ice cream (and more!). It was a sight to behold! The temptation was great. I observed senior citizens from our table and all about us, dash to the dessert tables and load up their plates -- and then go back for seconds! I smiled inwardly as I exerted my self-control (thanks to poker) and was satisfied to enjoy two small cookies with my coffee. *And I was so proud of myself!*

* * *

And What About Physical Health?

Playing poker is a rather sedentary activity. Right? You are seated at a table hour after hour. How can you possibly get any physical exercise? How can you say that playing poker is good for your physical health?

As a matter of fact, there are exercises you can do while sitting at the table. <u>Isometrics</u> is a system of exercises that involve the straining by contraction or stretching of muscles without significant bodily movements. In isometric exercises, one muscle or part of the body is pitted against another or against an immovable surface in a strong but motionless pressing, pushing, pulling, stretching, bending, or contraction. An example is pushing the palms of your hands against each other. Another rather simple isometric exercise is to grab the bottom of the seat of your chair while you are seated there, and pull upward. There are a wide variety of isometric exercises you can do while seated at the table, without disturbing others.

Remember, when you play by the four Basic Poker Rules (namely Rule #3), you will fold many more hands than you play. While you are observing and studying how your opponents are playing their hands during these periods, you can also use the time to do isometric exercises.

For example, grab the railing of the poker table with your hands and simultaneously press your feet against the base of the table or railing that surrounds the base; pull your hands backwards while you push your legs forward.

At the same time, suck in your stomach. You are exercising a variety of your muscles. *(Don't worry; the poker table is quite sturdy and won't move.)*

I have suffered in the past from injuries to my shoulders. One of the exercises my doctor had me do was simply to move my arm up to my chin, holding it horizontal with my other hand at the elbow, and then force my arm back toward the rear of my head. Hold that position for a few seconds, then repeat. This exercises and strengthens the shoulder muscles. I sometimes do that while the dealer is mixing the cards and preparing to deal the next hand. *(Of course it's just silly superstition on my part, but it seems whenever I do that simple exercise, I get dealt a good opening hand. Maybe the poker gods are rewarding me.)*

For the arthritis in one of my finger joints in my right hand, I do an exercise that the occupational therapist recommended: Use my other hand to press the arthritic finger against the palm of that hand; release it, and then press it to form a tight fist.

I used to suffer from a form of arthritis in my left hand where my fingers would suddenly lock up. It's very uncomfortable, almost painful. To prevent that occurrence, I use a "Magic Dani." It's like a wine-bottle cork, cylindrical in shape, about 1 3/4 in. long and 3/4 in. in diameter, that has been given a special treatment by my granddaughter, Danielle -- Dani, for short. *(She seems to have magical powers.)* Periodically, while sitting at the poker table, I will take a "Magic Dani" out of my pocket to use. I simply place the flat surfaces at the ends between one of my fingers and my thumb on the opposite end, and squeeze them against the "Magic Dani." I do that for each of my fingers, over and over again. *During my poker seminars at senior citizens groups, I've demonstrated and given "Magic Danis" to several other senior citizens who also suffer similar finger-joint problems, which appears to be fairly common. Several months after one of these seminars, one of the attendees contacted me to request another "Magic Dani" for her husband.*

Why birthdays are good for you:
The more you have, the longer you live!

The E-Word

There is no question that the E-word is the single most important factor for good physical health:

EXERCISE!

But you don't have to change into gym clothes and work up a sweat for an hour to get the exercise you need. The U.S. Surgeon General's Report on *Physical Activity and Health* suggests you can accumulate just 30 minutes of moderate-intensity physical activity several days a week -- not even every day. . .

A brisk walk is a good form of exercise. While playing poker, it is prudent to take a break once an hour or so; go to the restroom; get some fresh air. And, while you're at it, take a short 10-15 minute brisk walk. Swing your arms as you walk. Take some deep breaths of fresh air. It will also invigorate you, clear your head, make you more alert, and prepare you for another hour or two of concentrated poker playing -- hopefully winning poker play!

During your brisk walk, you might think about any intriguing hands or perhaps mistakes you may have made while playing a particular hand, so you can better learn the lesson from that experience. Also, think about your opponents at the table: What are their respective strengths and weaknesses? How should you play against each? Which ones do you need to be careful of? Why? Which ones can you easily bluff out? Who are the PokerSharks and who are the PokerPigeons? Should you try to change your seat to get to the left of a particularly aggressive or deceptive player?)

* * *

And It's Fun Too!

In closing,, I repeat what has been stated before:

It's great fun to be a winner!

➤ _____ ◄

Appendix

Folding Hands for Texas Hold'em

There are certain two-card combinations that should never be played pre-flop unless you are the big blind. You <u>may</u> want to stay in pre-flop with some of the medium-to-high-ranking "Fold" hands shown below if you are the small blind and the pot has not been raised.

Suited Combinations	Unsuited Combinations
Note: <u>Play</u> all suited combinations of A-X and K-X depending on position. The higher ranking hands — those where X is a ten or higher — may be played in any position; for the lower ranking hands, it is highly desirable to play these in middle-late positions relative to the betting sequence. **Fold with:** **Q-7 and below** **J-6 and below** **10-6 and below** **9-5 and below** **8-5 and below** **7-4 and below** **6-4 and below** **5-3; 5-2;** **4-3; 4-2; 3-2**	**Fold with:** **A-5 and below** **K-5 and below** **Q-9 and below** **J-9 and below** **10-8 and below** **9-7 and below** **8-6 and below** **7-6 and below** **6-5 and below** **5-4 and below** **4-3; 4-2; 3-2**

George 323 938-7023